William Howitt

The Mad War-Planet

And Other Poems

William Howitt

The Mad War-Planet
And Other Poems

ISBN/EAN: 9783744713047

Printed in Europe, USA, Canada, Australia, Japan

Cover: Foto ©Thomas Meinert / pixelio.de

More available books at **www.hansebooks.com**

THE MAD WAR-PLANET;

And Other Poems.

BY WILLIAM HOWITT.

"War is a game, which, were their subjects wise,
Kings would not play at."—COWPER's "TASK."

"The heart of the sons of men is full of evil, and madness is
in their heart while they live."—ECCLESIASTES ix. 3.

"Ognuno ha il suo ramo di Pazzia."—ITALIAN PROVERB.

LONDON:

LONGMANS, GREEN, READER, AND DYER,

PATERNOSTER ROW.

1871.

PREFACE.

DURING the past summer and autumn, whilst almost daily ascending the snow-clad mountains of Switzerland and Northern Italy : whilst gazing on their silent glaciers, traversing their noble forests, or listening to the sound of their rushing rivers, or to the musical cadences of their pastoral rills on their Alpine heights, in that wonderful health and vigour rarely conscious of fatigue, which are the result of temperance, physical activity, and the blessing of God, these poems have been written. Amid the peace of Nature in those glorious lands, the continual tidings of the incredible barbarities of war inflicted on each other by peoples calling themselves civilized and Christian, have stimulated me to make that solemn protest against such prodigious madness and crime, in this period of pretended enlightenment, which ought to be uttered by every man and woman who claim to be in their senses. Yet, so far from the astounding horrors of this war having caused European governments to pause in so diabolical a career, we see on all hands the signs of its indefinite extension. France fallen, Russia turns with renewed hope towards Turkey, and is making enormous preparations. No man can now say when or where this fury of bloodshed shall end. Who then shall affirm that the title of the chief poem of this volume is not most thoroughly and sorrowfully justified ?

The leading poem of this volume was commenced at Zurich in August, when society there was at a white heat of Prussianism. It was completed early in November, at Bellagio, on the Lake of Como.

I wish it to be distinctly understood that the theory of this poem is not put forth by me as a mere poetical one : but as a most sorrowful psychological fact, palpable on the face of all history. I hold that the Fall of Man was not simply a fall from innocence, but a plunge into the Satanic sphere, which, inasmuch as it is a separation from God, the centre of all truth and perception and measure of truth, and the source of all soundness of intellect as well as of goodness, is a condition of the loss of these, and therefore, necessarily of aberration and confusion, or in other words, of absolute and perpetual insanity. This insanity in the fallen hosts is demonstrated by the vain and incessant attempts to overthrow the order and happiness of the universe. The insanity of the human race, the consequence of its submergence into the Satanic, or abnormal sphere, is too indisputably and sorrowfully demonstrated by six thousand years of incessant bloodshed in every quarter of the globe, which no advance in knowledge or civilization diminishes, but which, on the contrary, seems to increase in horror and atrocity with the increase of intelligence. The only escape from this terrible condition of things, is, by an acceptance of Christianity in the fulness of its power and principle : but which no church, or body, except that of the Friends, has dared to assume and to rely upon.   The experiment of Penn in founding Pennsylvania was a complete proof of the soundness of their doctrine, that the consequence of literally accepted Christianity is the utter supersedence of War.

W. H.

ROME, *January* 15, 1871.

CONTENTS.

MINOR POEMS.

THE MAD WAR-PLANET.

CHAPTER I.

TIDINGS OF WAR.

CATTLE and sheep are daily led to slaughter,
And quietly they go ; and therefore men
Pronounce these beasts, the stupidest of things.
But if these creatures had the power of speech
What would they say of men ?   Their words would
   be,—
" These human herds are daily led to slaughter,
And quietly they go, for they are truly
The stupidest of things."
   So, sitting under shade of the beech woods,
Upon the breezy heights of Zürichberg,*

* The hill north of Zürich.

I

With all that marvellous scene of city and vale
Spread out before me, came these humbling thoughts.
  Oh ! beautiful that spot ! and beautiful
Transcendently that landscape, lake and town !
Around me rose the thousand pillared stems,
The blue sky glimpsing through their verdurous tops,
Which, all astir with the quick, living air,
Quivered and soughed, and to the radiant sun
Whispered, in the old language of the woods,
Of myriad-creatured life 'neath gladsome boughs.
And through this gentle, ever-tossing sea
Of foliage, the sun-light showering down
In golden luxury, and in scattered gleams
On leafy mosses and on hoary ground,
Made the shade light, yet left it still a shade,
Solemn, and sweet with soul-embracing peace.
  And fronting these, in the illumined grass,
The wild flowers nodded, and the wild thyme
        breathed
Its spicy essence : grass-hopper and bee
Hummed, and basked chithering in the bliss of life.
  And all a-down those slopes of marshalled vines,

And fruit-trees bowed beneath their prodigal loads,

The peasants' houses and the peasant bands,

Father and mother and proudly helping child,

Made one great picture of the wealth of God

Poured stintlessly upon the fields of men.

And in the valley's heart, that dense, great town

With all its thickly-clustered, ruddy roofs,

Its ancient towers and spires and learned halls,

Its homes of mercy and its marts of trade;

Its mill-wheels dashing through its emerald floods,

The hammer's clang, the factory's columned smoke,

Its steam tracks running out to other lands,

And all its white-walled suburbs interspersed

With gardens, tree-crowned knolls, and orchard
    plots—

What a broad, busy nest of breathing life!

City! that throwest forth thy populous arms

On all sides, as if bent to gather in

The country's wealth : thou vale extending far

Westward, with all thy villages and cots

Mid gently-swelling hills: thou Uetliberg,

Southward ascending with thy forest steeps :

Lake, that for many a league dost brightly gleam,
One liquid plain of beauty, bordered round
With rural paradises, hamlets and spires,
White flashing out amid their vineyard hills,
Like sails upon a green and billowy sea;
Ye mountains closing in the distant East,
Ye craggy ramparts of a giant world,
Wild peaks, sky-dwellers amid ancient snows—
Slumberers and dreamers in eternal space—
Together, in one concrete round, ye form
A scene where man, upon the base of God,
Has raised a platform of industrious art,
And built an amphitheatre of love,
And shown in visible and substantial shape
As God himself of old did herald it,
" Peace upon earth and good-will unto men."

And yet !—Ah yet !—how slight a circumstance;
How shallow, and how pitiful a cause,
Or even no cause at all, but wanton will,
A lust of power, or discord strangely raised
On shadowy, misty grounds, how none could say,
Might bring a murderous, maniac multitude,

The sons of death, the ministers of hell,
Calling themselves the sons of the good God,
The warriors of the Prince of Peace himself,
The smiting hosts of Him who said " Smite not :"
The murdering hosts of Him who said " Kill not ;
But bless and curse not : evermore do good,
Even to your foes ; leave vengeance unto God !"
  And these infuriate liars to their creed
Might drive the startled peasants from their ploughs
And from their ever-busy spades and hoes,
And trample down their corn; and burn their homes;
And fling into the living, pulsing town
Infernal masses of destructive metals
Charged with Satanic fires,—crashing in roofs
Of palace and church and hospital and house ;
And on the breast of the affrighted mother,
Smiting the clinging, sunny-headed child
Into a bloody horror : works of peace
And hoarded wealth of art and trade, might send
Blazing and hissing through the fire-flaked reek
Into the skies.
        " No, never can such deeds,"

Numbers exclaim, " dishonour times like these !
·Most Christian, wise and civilizéd times !
Times all ensouled with knowledge and with thought,
And god-like sentiment, and Christian zeal."

    Alas ! how many times has Christian zeal,
So-styled, made havoc in this very town.
As in that terrible night, the Murder Night,*
.So called by history ; or, when, still worse,
Faith against faith contending, Zürich and Basle,
In deadly strife with the Old Forest States,
Most Catholic.   How many times have hordes
Of Christian-tonguéd men, made demon work
Throughout this mountain land, Burgund and
        French
And Austrian ; canton how oft with canton,
Papal and Protestant ; whose creeds were peace,
Who as their common Lord did claim the Lamb,
Ravaged and ruined landscapes fair as this ;
And left huge misery in the name of God.

    And what ! this very hour, and on the bounds
Almost of this same land, two nations wage

* See p. 11.

A deadly war to win what neither needs,

More realms, more peoples, having realms immense,

And myriad peoples, and all wealth and goods

That nations want; and over lands as fair,

Bounded by mountains beautiful as these,

With brilliant cities and perfected arts,

And populations loud with song and joy

But yesterday, they rain their iron hail,

And slaughter men like beasts, and drench the vines

On the sweet sun-lit hills with human blood :

Revelling in murder and in demon hate, ·

As though no gospel ever had been preached,

No Son of God, descending, given the law

Of love and peace, as the One Father's will ;

As though they never had professed this faith ;

Had never knelt in solemn vow, and sworn

Before the altar of the King of Peace

Him to obey, and from their inmost hearts

To live his life, and love as he had loved ;

Self-love in brother-love quenching, till the earth

Was with itself at one, and one with heaven.

In vain ! through thousand upon thousand years

Mankind has lived, and learned a vast amount
Of wise and curious things, but never yet
Has learnt to live in peace, and to enjoy
The good which God has showered upon their heads.

Oh, monstrous ! Oh ! fact beyond all credence,
Did not our own eyes see it. Saw we not
Its hideous presence, ghastly, wan, and dark,
Before us, like some portent from the hells.

And whence, ye shrewd philosophers,—ye men
With powers profound to fathom man's deep heart ;
To analyze his motives, and make clear
The darkest problems of his complex life ;—
Whence the enigma of this knowing world ?
This fair, this bounteous world ; this world where
    sun,
Earth, air, and water, 'neath the rule of God,
Make a bright paradise for man to mar ;
Make all that soul can wish, or brain conceive
For happiness and strength, glory, and work
Fruitful of blessing ; all, from time to time,
Whirled into chaos by this human god,—
Torn, trodden, rent and damned with direst woes ;

And murder made its rule, and misery
Its queen, enthroned on palpitating hearts
That murder has not stilled.   Oh ! mighty men,
Powerful to frame nice theories of sense
And of man's inner being ; skilful to class
And catalogue whatever can be found
Upon the earth, or under ; able to weigh
In metaphysic balance every cause
Except the First, who is not in your plan.

    Tell me, ye pioneers of occult truth, .
Though but the truth of matter ; bold explorers
Of the dynamic springs of this round globe ;
Torturers of atoms, analysts of light,
Capturers of force and essences, who strip
Sunlight of substance, naming it vibration ;
Ye men to whom the plastic source of life
Is soon to yield its secret ; lords of fact,—-
Tell me whence is the cause of this war-curse ?

    Alas ! 'tis not in you ! nor in your field.
This arrow flies beyond you, and stands fixed
In the grey region of primeval time :
Beneath tradition's lightning-riven clouds.

'Tis not your theme, but mine ; and I will now
Open this casket of Pandoric truth—
Draw forth the mystic rolls of a past world ;
Produce the oracles of days when God
Gave wisdom, and philosophers were not ;
Uttering immortal truths, that in the souls
Of the first men took deathless root, and went
With them from land to land, from age to age,
Shining like stars amid the pagan glooms,
Heralds of coming life, and worship-laws
To every nation's sages, till they met
And culminated on the head of Christ—
The Way, the Truth, the Life for evermore !

NOTE TO CHAPTER I.

The Murder Night of Zürich was the result of a conspiracy instigated by Austria in 1350, then the over-bearing neighbour of Switzerland. Austria was in possession of Rapperschwyl at the head of the lake ; and contrived to win over a number of the citizens of Zürich, to the betrayal of their city. The conspiracy was discovered through a baker's boy, and the conspirators were surprised, and thirty-seven of them brought out and beheaded before their houses. Brun, the burgomaster, determined to attack Rapperschwyl, but he was met on the way by 4,000 Austrians, and disgracefully ran away : but Sir Rudiger Maness took the command, and defeated the Austrians at Tätwyl ; seized six of their banners, and returned in triumph.

CHAPTER II.

As when some lordly house stands festively

With all its corridors and open doors,

Its windows glittering in the morning sun,

Its fanes and pinnacles ablaze on high,

Its marble steps, as if inviting feet,

Its fountains quivering in dancing light,

Its gardens, sun and shade, verdure and tint

Of many and intense glories, breathing forth

Airs of entrancing sweetness; and within

Its halls and galleries with statues fair,

And paintings from the hands oɪ mightiest skill,

Blazoning the walls with the great men and deeds

That were the life and livers in the past:

And all its noble rooms for daily use,

Its silken chambers and retreats of ease,

Rich everywhere with whatsoever art

And wealth can give ; its,saintly chapel carved

And painted, and made proudly rich and quaint

With all the mastery of great architect

And artist of each kind : with organ set

Ready to shout aloud the praise of God—

As when such princely residence stands thus

Waiting and listening—or seeming so—

With many auditories, and a hush

Of eager·expectation on its walls—

And yet there comes no guest—no honoured lord

Leading his bride unto her beauteous home,

Herself all beauty ; and around a throng

Of jocund friends in the excess of life,

And menials running as on wingéd feet

To meet their will half spoken, or divined—

So stood the new earth waiting its first lords.

    Man ! at thy birth upon this beauteous world,—

How fair thy fortunes !   How divine thy lot !

A world more sweet had never brightened space.

A world more rich in loveliness and store

Of all delights; a paradise of bliss;
A home immortal in the immortal skies;
A heaven on heaven's own frontiers, loved of God!
Beholding which, the bright, immortal hosts
From spheres of innermost heaven in wonder stood,
And all the morning stars together sang,
And all the Sons of God shouted for joy.

    This was the radiant point in earth's dim course;
This was its bright and violet spot, whose light
Thrown from her happy surface, still has shone
The after-glow of man's descended sun : ˙
And lived and lives for ever in our dreams.
This was the blest poetic time, so brief,
Which all the seers and bards of every age,
And every clime and nation celebrate,
As the great golden age, when the high gods
Walked with our fathers, and the world had peace.

    Yes, as the Hebrew prophet-annalist
Proclaims divinely, God himself did walk
With his first children of this human globe
Rejoicing in his work, so heavenly fair;
And poured into their minds the living stream

Of truths and knowledges a thousand-fold.

As their own consciousness it flowed within,

For their pure, half ethereal bodies drank

The lore of heaven, the spirit-speech of God,

Fully and freely, as the diamond drinks

And burns with light : or as the crystal pane

Transmits the solar beams.   But quick the change !

  There is a Power, mighty, but not all-mighty,

Of force yet second only to those Powers

Create of God, and made the autocthones

And rulers of great spheres, in his own realm

Of worlds innumerous, wheeling through all space.

It is a power of forfeited allegiance,

Of fiercest rebel mind, rabid with hate ;

Bent to destroy, disorganize and curse

All that is good and lovely, loving and kind.

For in abjuring God, God has abjured

Him and his followers : having rent the tie

Which knit him to the fountain of all life

And all perfection, he has nothing left

But what is opposite, and dark and crooked,

And furious and malign.   His vital force

Lives undiminished, but it is a force
Cunning as strong, and base as it is subtle.
And with it he has worked in quenchless hate
Since the heavens closed their amethystine gates
Abrupt upon him.   And his legions foul
Wander where'er permitted through God's worlds
In the fond hope that they can scatter death.

This is the dread condition of this Prince,
Who is the maniac of the universe,
Hoping against all proof of time, to wreak
His malice on the perfect peace of God,
And on the power of God invincible.

Far off the sense of this young, radiant world
And of its new-created beings, fell on him
By telegraphic life, which is in spirits
Unlimited by time, or space, or law :
And with a wish he stood upon its soil.
And saw the founders of another race,
To spring and multiply beyond the power,
Even of archangels in their keenest thought,
To calculate.   He saw them wear the forms
Of his lost heaven, and saw the tribes of heaven

Visiting them, and giving them their love.

And with the sight came, lightning-like, resolve

To blast and ruin this great scheme of God.

We need not paint the means by which he wrought

This base achievement, and sent out a joy

Fierce and delirious through the many hells.

We have it in the diction of those times.

We have it limned and traced in imagery

Primevally symbolic, quaint and dim,

But not the less ensouled by the great fact.

By subtlest flattery; by the fond ambition

Infused in man, which had destroyed himself,

He woke the curse in earth which rules it still.

For it was needed only to effect

The severance of the loyalty of man

From God, and down he fell, body and soul,

Into the madness of the infernal life.

Losing the life and wisdom of the Lord,

He sank baptised in the dark frenzy-floods

. Of life antagonist, perplexed, distorted,

And into darkness traversed but by light

Which is itself delusion.   Heir no longer

2

Of God's celestial truth and perfect vision,
Man became heir of all the infernal guiles.
He was inoculate with the virulence
Of the inverted principles of being : filled
With the delirium of the maniac spheres,
Whose madness is their wisdom, and whose love,
Acidified to hate, burns and destroys,
As in its primal sweetness it gave life.
It was a fury turning upside down
The inward man, and inside out his aims :
So that he looked on death as truest good
And murder as true glory ; and to ruin
As the sublimest attribute of heroes.

At this dread change, heaven shifted far away,
And the deep hells rose phantom-like and swept
Over the earth in eddies of dismay ;
And filled it with an orgasm of disease,
And sights and cries of anguish and despair.

A shock and shudder went through all its frame :
And over all its skies came tempest clouds,
And thunders bellowed round it, and wild winds
Hissed forth a voice of dolor.   Beast on beast,

And bird on bird, and insect upon insect,

From high to low, from greatest to the smallest,

Raved with the madness; drank each other's blood,

And battened on the bodies of the weak.

Terror and death usurped the reign of peace;

Rapidly worked the curse from the abyss;

Rapidly spread the ruin with the race.

Its first-fruits fell from rancour's Upas boughs.

Its deeds were deeds as of the damned themselves.

The first-born man arose and slew his brother.

For envy and the lust of others' goods,

Raged in the earth, which overflowed with goods

Beyond all power to reap them : and mad greed

Grew from the subterranean heat of Hades,

As poison weeds spring in volcanic soil.

Fast as the race did multiply, grew crime,

And lust and robbery and murder ruled,

And made their perpetrators chiefs and kings.

For it was part of the stupendous power

Of Satan so to stupefy the brain

Of the great, grovelling multitude, that they

Should worship their destroyers, and fall down

And lick the feet that waded through their gore :
And make themselves the slaves of those strong brutes,
To kill and desolate at their command.
Ay, thousands upon thousands yielded up
Their liberty and life to one sole man,
And made themselves machines of wholesale death,
And massacred their kind at one sole will,
And hailed the monster maniac as a god.

Madness enormous ! madness past belief !
Were it not earth's great story through all time ;
Were it not raging now, and more and more.

Adam's infected blood produced a race
Of murderers : and Eve, feeding upon her woe,
A race of mourners : these twain multiplied,
And through their long descent still multiply,
The sons of death and daughters of distress.
Those compass sea and land to shed men's blood :
These sit at home and shed unheeded tears.

But why retell what God himself has told ?
Why echo faintly his immortal tome,
Whose words were streamed through pens of living
     fire,

And through the fire-baptiséd souls of seers
Who held aloft through time the beacon-lights
Of his eternal truth before mankind ?
Once and for ever they have told earth's tale,
Fallen and maddened by a murderous spell.
There we have all its struggles and its woes.
How the whole race ran frantically mad,
And grovelled in impurity, and smote
Deliriously each other ; and blasphemed
Him, their Creator, till he swept them out
By his avenging flood. How then he chose
Man after man, as of a saner mind,
To renovate the race and guide anew.
But vainly : for the potent curse raged on,
And Satan gloried in his trophied wrongs ;
And finding earth's impressible clime, than hell's
More genial, and more kindred to his views
Than those below, his seat he planted there.
There ruled in demon glory, and in work
Incessant to undo the works of God.

  And from his hells beneath he gave the name
Of that which he had made it, unto earth,

And that which soon throughout the universe
Became its designate—the Hell of Blood.
And every age throughout six thousand years
Has justified that name, and has allowed,
Even to Satan, in this instance, Truth.

But in celestial regions it is termed
The Mad War-Planet, whose ensanguined disk
Wears the deep dye of blood; and rain of blood,
To angel vision, trickles from its sky.

To the perfected tribes of peace and love
Its presence is a horror, and the scent
That to their delicate organs floats far off,
Is redolent of gore, and sickens them.
And sometimes, as from world to beauteous world,
They voyage for fresh knowledge and delight,
In God's most infinitely varied works,
When they perceive this dwelling of red discord,
Backward they turn and flee amain, until
They feel the ethereal atmosphere is freed
From pungent taint of its miasmal death.

And thus, what God created fair, and still
Warms with his sun, and fructifies with life,

Satan has made his human slaughter-house,

And his poor victims, all untaught by time,

Still dream his teachings glory ; with red hands

Turn on each other, battle, groan, and die.*

---

* " For this the conqueror rears
The arch of triumph ! and for this the tears
And blood of earth flow on as they have flowed,
An universal deluge, which appears
Without an ark for wretched man's abode,
And ebbs but to reflow !   Renew thy rainbow, God !"
Childe Harold, Canto iv., p. 164.

CHAPTER III.

THE WORKING OF THE CURSE.

THE mystery of evil ! of all themes
The earliest, most discussed, most intricate !
Theme by most ancient sages in all lands,—
By shrewdest analysts of human mind,—
By the philosophers in nature's laws
Most versed and intimate,—by anchorites
Spending their weary lives in deserts grey,
To tear the clinging evil from their flesh,
And sunk for ever in a trance profound,
Digging and delving for the great solution.
Hoarest of all enigmas ! more abstruse
Than ever Sphinx propounded, or was guessed
By any Œdipus,—still the great theme
That sets the learned masters of our age,

The metaphysic athletes of the schools,

The theologic skill of every church,

Lightly at nought,—we seek not to explore.

Let it remain unfathomed !   'Tis enough

For us to know that He who planned and built

This mighty universe, this maze of worlds,

Infinite in number and extent ; scarce less

Incomprehensible than is Himself

Is clearly infinitely good and wise,

And mighty too as He is good and wise :

And granting this, we know that what He plans

He will conduct unto its proper end.

   He who is infinite needs not that we,

Finite, and cribbed in flesh, and of to-day,

Should comprehend Him, but should watch and

     wait,

And seeing how his blessings hold their march,

Should love Him, and adore Him till the time

When He shall call us nearer, and reveal

More of his purpose.   Hitherto we know

Not our own being ; not our birth and growth

Symmetrical, nor how our sentient mind

Commences and progresses, and stores up

Harvests of knowledge in a little pulp

That we call brain ; and yet we would presume

To know the ways and aims of Him who knows

Neither beginning, limit, law, nor end.

    Yet still through time, and still in every nation,

Men have been asking why this orb perverse,

Created beautiful by God, and so pronounced

As " very good," having received a hurt,

As it would seem so mortal, should not be

Re-cast and purged from its calamity,

And permeating guilt ; and man, its lord,

So basely rendering up his loyalty,

And yielding him the slave of hostile powers,

Should not be sunk annihilate, and life

More worthy planted on his heritage ?

And why this evil Power, the source of all

The crime and sorrow of earth, should not be bound,

Or sunk with man in one deservéd doom

Of dark extermination : so that earth

Should do its mission in perpetual joy,

And live and honour God in perfect peace ?

But He who doth desire a noble race
Of conscious souls, in will and action free,
And not mere slaves or puppets, knows right well
That without trial there can be no strength.
That those untaught by evil cannot reach
The perfect knowledge of good.   That a new race
Born to free-will must freely stand exposed
To the assaults of evil, even as men.

 Thus much we may perceive that God has
  deemed
Trial of those, whom he at length would call
To heavenly life, as indispensable,
Assayment as of gold in furnace fires.
And that the powers of evil bent to undo .
His will and works, are made by Him to do
That which they would not, and perfect them more.

 And this we know and feel as living truth,
That what God has created, He must love,
And will love on for ever : love through all,
And never can forsake.   That through all stains
And degradations, he will see his own
In the lost creature, and will claim it too.

He cannot suffer any evil power
To mar his labours, save for a brief space
That he may bring them forth more fair and clear.
He cannot lose an atom of his own :
But will sum up the tale of all his lives
At the great end, and show to all his hosts
That what he planned is done : and that no Power
Is sovereign but himself.   That when his Son,
Love of his love, and worker of his will,
Shall give up all to him, and he shall be
Then all in all, so all shall be in Him.

And those who cannot climb to this great truth,
Glorious and godlike, worthy the Most High,
See but a particle of the vast whole
In seeing earth, and bear not in their mind
That he has other worlds in endless train,   .
Where he can discipline and purify
And perfect souls, till they reflect himself.

So from the first he gave not up the earth
Though fallen and rebel, but at once announced
That he would save it through his matchless
      patience,

As infinite in him as are they all,—
His attributes divine.   That his dear Son
Should take the form of man, and he in him
With all the Godhead working, should restore
His spiritual life in full; and he would give
Unto the woman who had been deceived
By the arch-serpent the sublime redress
To crush his dragon head; and by her seed
To build anew the glory of her race.

   So ever in the world's delirious tribes
Has God in Christ been ever more at work
Healing and saving, and by silent law
Drawing the sad and suffering unto him.
But this, in the coarse turmoil of the nations,
Passed little noticed by the common eye,
And empire after empire in old times
Rose and grew mighty, fell and disappeared.
For they had little in them but brute strength
And pride of war, and lust of lawless power.
And other nations rose, idolatrous,
But in their darkness showing lines of light
And mastering science, scanning the wide heavens,

And having speculations most profound
Upon the soul and destinies of man.
And knowing primal truths, and writing them,
As they were given by God to the first seers,
But not to culminate except in Christ
In all their strength and concentrated light.

   So Egypt, India, and the quaint Cathay,
The China of our speech, dropped genuine truths,
But few and isolated from the pens
Of Trismegistus, Laotze or Fo,
From dreamy speech of Brahma or Buddhu,
Or Persian Zerduz, worshipper of fire,
But none of these great peoples by their arts,
Or by their loftiest lore, could break the spell
Of Satan's giant madness, and they shed
Oceans of blood, and worshipped bloody fiends.

CHAPTER IV.

INFLUENCE OF PAGAN LITERATURE.

BUT fairer far and greater than them all,
Not in their numbers, for they were but few,
But great in vigour of expansive soul,
Rose the Greek nations in a later day.
For they were organized in beauty's mould
Personal and spiritual. They were full of grace
And full of intellect blent sensuously
With an intensity of yearning life,
With all its vivid pleasures and desires,
Its fiery passions, loves and sudden hates,
Surging and burning in volcanic breasts.
    Beauty they saw before them, day and night,
But beauty chiefly in the human form,
And out of it they wrought the elements

To gods and goddesses, and worshipped them,
Thus worshipping themselves in sculptured shapes.
They deified humanity and made
Gods their own counterparts idealized.
Gods beauteous, strong, lascivious and proud—
And so they worshipped their own faults and crimes
Disguised in hues of loftiest poetry,
And in the majesty of noblest art.
With restless quest their philosophic men
Pursued the latent springs of human thought
Unto their source, and framed deep theories
Of man, and of his subtle mechanism,
Material and mental, with a host
Of dreams and myths of whence he had arisen :
And how in time he grew to what he was.
They had great healers, men of deathless names :
And others who taught reason's perfect rules ;
And others great in measure and in number ;
And others great in speech, whereby they rose
To eloquence of sweet or stormy power,
That made the listeners plastic to its spell,
As is the giant ocean to the wind.

But their large idiosyncracies and gifts,
Their ardent faculties combined or single,
Yielded the sovereignty to power of song
Most marvellous, and seeming more than human.
In every form gushed forth the stream of soul,
In verse of every character and tone.
Their lyrists sang the songs of love and wine,
And shrilled forth trumpet notes exciting war.
Their dramatists made woe and tragic deed,
And the fierce rush of passions, strong as death,
Career through life, rivers of liquid fire.
And kindled sympathies whose mournful sweep
Struck through the world, and reached to heaven
        and hell,—
Themes that yet thrill with wonder and hot tears.
    But far above them all, in meteor light,
Arose one mighty man, one kingly name
Of rhythmic genius, blazing forth, a sun
Amid a host of swiftly paling stars.
Homer, that blind old bard into whose mind
God had poured light, and strength of boundless
        vision.

3

Giving him eyes within his ample breast
That ran through all things, and made all his own.
God crowned him with a power which was the life
Of whatsoever moved in the wide earth,
Or in the ocean wastes ; and what he sung
Received a charmed existence, that no time
Could touch, or change, or weaken.   In his lays
We see the lofty walls of Ilium girt
By Grecian hosts : see Helen looking down
On the fierce strife that grew from out her beauty.
See all those mighty chiefs of deathless name,
Battle and shout regardless of the flight
Of vastest ages ; shield dashed against shield,
And sword and spear in deadly combattance,
Active as when the poet gave them life,
Thus to war on for ever on Troy's plain.

But woe to human kind from that great song !
For God's rich gift in the Homeric soul
Satan converted to a spring of death
More deadly, more prolific of dire ills
Than every other cause and force malign
Bearing on man in his disastrous course.

For Greece was all one field of martial flame;
Destruction was its glory, and its pride
Fed on the poison growths of this lost world.
On quick resentment of the slightest wrongs,
And on revenge as prompt, it built its fame.

The soul of Homer was the soul of Greece.
Whatever lived in Greece was life in him;
And in his wondrous song he gathered all
Its themes of admiration.   Hence he made
His hero beautiful and brave; with friends
Friendly, and prone to love; but to his foes
The full embodiment of wrath and pride.
And blazing as a god in victory's car
He bade him stand, the worship of the world!

And thus unconsciously this glorious bard
Became the prophet and the prince of death;
And by his chanting voice has slain more men,
And spread more dreadful ruin than all kings
And military butchers, famed for blood.

So raged the nations for four thousand years.
No spot of the round world was left exempt.
From age to age the curse sent forth its hordes,

Led by the demigods of wholesale carnage
Empowered by hell's great sorcerer to destroy.

From land to land the iron bands of Rome
Spread, and laid low the pride of Eastern kings.
Their stalwart troops singing the rude old songs
Of their republican and rugged days;
And later, grown imperial and proud,
Hymning the lays of Virgil on their march.
For this pale ghost of Homer had the power
To edge the sword of conquest in their hands,
Whilst they subdued the nations to their yoke,
And having wasted them still sought for more :
Pushing their mercenary legions on
Through the deep swamps and melancholy woods
Of Gaul, Germania, and the British Isles
To the bleak mountains of the Pictish north.
And where, in southern climes, and savage lands
Reigned ignorance and sloth, there still flowed
        blood ;
And the war madness cursed all human kind.

CHAPTER V.

At length the time so long beheld by seers,
Many and various in their gifts and styles
And breadth of inward vision, but on one
Divinest theme, one-voiced,—the birth of Christ
Into the world, and into man's own life ;—
The time had come, and earth beheld her Lord.
 But not as human nature, proud and blind,
Looked for him did he come. Not as a king
With heaven's own host surrounded, to cast down .
Earth's monarchs from their thrones, himself to
  reign.
For force had long enough held sway below,
And force is death to every phase of freedom.
He would free men from the old tyrannies

Of mind and person ; but this perfect freedom
Must spring, and grow, and spread without restraint.

    Nor did he come as kin to any caste
Exclusively, as royal or high born,
Though son of David by far-off descent—
Lineage no longer regal, nor of note.
He would not that the blood of priest or noble
Should be the quickener of his mortal frame,
For then the favoured caste had claimed to be
Heaven's own elect, and over every other
Had lorded it with plea of right divine.
Nor would he enter love's conjugal sphere
And become founder of a special race,
For then these had been held as demigods,
And had been worshipped with fanatic zeal,
·And a more awful tyranny sprung thence
Than earth, so wed to miseries, ever knew.

    Nor would he lend to wealth, or casual power
The sanction of his birthright ; but he came
Simple and poor, and claiming no distinction
But as the Son of God and Son of Man :
The Son of Man at large in one pure kinship

To every living soul in human form.

Nor would he study in college or in school
Lest they should claim to be the agencies
And causal springs of his divinest lore.

Nor would he teach in man's erected fanes
Rather than in the temples built of God.
On the free mountains and on greensward slopes,
Or by the wayside tracks of common life,
Or in the busy market-place, or 'neath
The roof despised of publican and sinner,
He loved to sit and teach as guest and friend.

Thus independent, thus from every tie,
Guild or profession, holding himself free,
He calmly trod the paths of poverty,
And chose his friends and prophets from the poor.

Thus from the highest scat in heaven, he chose
To take the lowest seat in sinful earth.
For his great work was to reverse the whole
Of earth's philosophy and laws of life ;
To cast its glory down as a fool's dream ;
To root its maxims out as false and foul ;
To show its wisdom,—barren vanity,

And its gross heart a fetid charnel-house.

And all that soaring spirit and high mood

Which they thought glory,—fiery, quick resentment,

And high disdain of insult, and revenge,

He stamped as Adam's blood, morbid self-love,

And impotence of temper born of Hades.

And on the ruins of this rotten state

He raised meekness and gentleness, the strength

Of the strong heavens, a heroism sublime,

Because it could resist, not outward foes

And outward wrongs alone, but the dark power

That lurks within and irritates the heart ;

And is the source of every petty strife,

And in its climax is the fire of war.

That which to Grecian mind was mean and base,

Looked cowardice and cravenhood, he showed

Was the high type of heroism, the soul

Of noblest magnanimity, and root

Of god-like grace and virtue.   And forthwith

To demonstrate the heroism of the skies,

He took a little child, and taught that those

Who would win heaven must be a child in heart,

All gentleness and love.   And to the sage
Coming by night to learn the way of life,
He spoke the startling word, that none should see
The kingdom of the blest but those reborn
From Adam's wrathful nature into God's.
He blessed the meek, and showed himself the way
Of the true hero, which was not to kill
Your foes, but bless them ; not to render evil
For evil, blow for blow, but ever make
Divinest recompense of evil with good.

And so our blessed Lord, the first true hero,
The pattern of all power in gentleness,
The patient, loving, blessing, perfect man,
Walked through the world diffusing round him good
And suffering insult : yet with quenchless love,
Showering out benefactions ; calling death
Back to new life, through sickness breathing health.

By his great miracles he showed the world
His title to the Son of the Most High :
But still more clearly by the god-like power
By which he could endure the basest wrong.
And thus he lived and died, sealing his truth

In his own blood, and by his farewell, blessing.

    Such was the grace with which this maniac world
Received a ministering God.   But when he rose,
And burst the tomb, and took his way on high,
Then, for a moment, broke the dark delusion.
The sons of men awoke, wept, and adored :
And all the warmth of heaven was felt on earth.
And there was wondrous opening of hearts ;
And the enraptured multitude rejoiced,
And walked together in a dream of love :
And spent their lives and substance for the Lord.

    But brief was this bright reign of gospel truth.
Back came the surging waves of Satan's sea ;
Back came the spirit of pagan and of Jew ;
Back came the priestly dominance of each,
With all their lust of power, and blinding arts.
There stood Christ's sun-bright words—"God is a
       spirit,
And men must worship Him in spirit and truth."
But these black spectres of an out-worn time,
Declared that man should worship him with robes ;
With yards of gaudy cloths and tissue of gold ;

With ceremonies gross and darkling creeds.

And the old temples of exploded gods,

They re-baptised, and others built in name

Of the Lord Jesus, knowing that the heavens

Were his great temple.   How he sate abroad,

And, in the simple majesty of truth,

Taught all men truth, and made them free of it.

   But these declared that they alone should teach,

Having some charter, which they never showed,

For binding truth again in cleric bonds,—

God's truth, which like God's winds is limitless !

And in their temples, these false sons of peace

Hung up aloft the banners of red Moloch,

And blest the instruments and acts of murder.

   And last, the subtlest artifice of hell,

The crowning triumph of Satanic art,

The war-fomenting literature of Greece,

The spirit of Homer and his kindred bards,

The spirit of Virgil and of martial Rome,

Was made the mental food of Christian youth.

Made indispensable to all who sought

To be the teachers, lawgivers, and priests,—

The governors and guides of Christendom.
So that through all the years of opening youth,
The vivid years, in which the heart and soul
Receive their tone and texture, and are wrought
To the determinate fashion of their life,—
The poison virus of lascivious gods,
Should take the place of Christ's philosophy—
Should be instilled and filtered through and through
Till it had drenched each nerve, and filled each pore
Of the internal man, and thus sent forth
The world's preparéd teachers, one and all,
The heralds of red war from age to age.

So now, ye peoples deeming yourselves Christians,
But in the sight of God, ye pagan realms,
Behold your work! behold the natural fruits
Of your false tree of knowledge! Ye have made
Of human life, a concrete pagan mass,—
Pagan and anti-Christian to the core,
With but the flimsiest film of Christian skin.
Till Satan laughs amongst his jeering fiends,
And asks—

" Where is their Christ? They worship him

In hollow form, but they are wholly mine.

Christ says that his are known to all by love.

But they have not a mark of love, or Christ.

It is not love to kill and to lay waste

The fields and dwellings of their fellow-men.

It is not love to frame machines of death,

And scatter agonies of fiercest kinds ;

And massacre their thousands day by day.

These are my works, and these are what they do,

And shall do at my bidding.   Mark my power !

  " There sits a man, learned, and wise, and good

In the world's judgment.   He abounds with views

Of knowledge and of progress.   He has penned

Marvellous volumes on the social state,

And on the brightening future of mankind.

He but to-day has lectured unto thousands

In a vast theatre, with views so broad

That thundered-forth applauses shook the hall.

And now he sits at home.   He has dined well,

And with his wife conversed on man's advance.

And thus he sits, a child upon his knee,

And his fair consort soothes him with her songs,

And with sweet music : and his ample breast
Is warm with love and pure philanthropy.

   " But hark ! a trumpet speaks, and up he starts !
A fire is in his eye and in his breast ;
And hastily he dons his murder-coat,
And his long murder-knife, yclept a sword,
He girds upon him : and away he speeds,
And with a gathering host of other maniacs,
Men excellent at home, and in sound mind,
Is metamorphosed to a raging fiend.
He casts philanthropy and glowing views
Of human progress to the winds, and stands
Ready to kill, and 'neath relentless feet
Trample the arts and hopes that he adores.

   " Look out, ye so-called Christians ! cast a view
From end to end of Europe.   How is this ?
Ye call yourselves the sons of Christ and peace,
And yet ye are at war ; or armed for war.
Millions are ready for the work of death.
How then can these be Christians ?   'Tis a lie
Monstrous and gross before the face of God
And of the shuddering heavens.   The work is mine !"

NOTE TO CHAPTER V.

THE LITERATURE OF GREECE AND ROME.

IF any one will take his New Testament and examine what is the standard of Christianity as there laid down by its Divine Founder, and will then look round him on this present world of ours, he will soon see that we are just where the moralists, the poets, the dramatists, of Greece and Rome, placed their world in the scale of ethics. And why so? Simply because we educate our children still in the Paganism of Aristophanes and Juvenal. We do it, and always have done it, diligently, uniformly, and thoroughly. We beat Paganism into our children, and expect them to turn out Christians. We used to put young sweeps up chimneys, and might as well have expected them to wave their brush from the chimney-pot with clean faces and ungrimed shirts. We have done with that; but we always did and do put our young men through the sinks of Paganism, and expect them to emerge saints.

These very Pagan writers themselves warn you in a thousand places of the inevitable consequences of the first teachings of youth. Habit, *we* say, is *second* nature ; but the old Pagans seemed to think that it

became the first, foremost, and only nature. We could
quote a volume from Plato, from Menander, and his
imitator, Terence, from Seneca, Lucian, Horace, and
the rest of them, to prove that what you sow in your
children you are sure to reap.

> "———— Dociles imitandis
> Turpibus et pravis omnes sumus."—JUVENAL.

But if you want to know what the ancients thought
of education read the whole fourteenth Satire of
Juvenal.

> "———— Cum septimus annus
> Transierit puero, nondum omni dente renato,
> Barbatos licet admoveas mille inde magistros,
> Hinc totidem————."

That is, when your boy has passed his seventh year
and has not yet renewed his teeth, you may give him
a thousand learned masters if you will, but it will be
all the same. But if this be the case at the end of
seven, what will it be at the end of seventeen? How
is it, then, that the Society for the Suppression of Vice
has not turned its attention to the works used in all
our national and other seminaries, as the text books
in Greek and Latin? They explore Holywell Street
diligently, and bring forward books and pictures
destructive of public morals for condemnation, yet
they never turn a single glance on Westminster or
Harrow, or Eton or Rugby, or a thousand other
schools, where the children of the higher and middle

classes are daily and regularly indoctrinated with Paganism, and this in its most obscene and unchristian forms. Lactantius, in his day, declared that it had been impossible to the heathen, however educated or civilised, to comprehend true virtue, much less to be virtuous, because their gods were set before them as examples of every species of violence, injustice, lasciviousness, adultery, and crimes unnameable. He especially mentions the books of Homer and Virgil as abounding with all these indecencies and monstrosities, as fraught from beginning to end with the spirit of war, of aggression, of physical violence, of sensuality, and of a turgid and intolerable pride. Yet what are the books now employed in all our schools in the teaching of the two languages which are deemed absolutely essential to every man of education? Precisely these very same books. Homer, Virgil, Terence, Ovid, Horace, and the like, are the books which are expected to be daily in the hands of all our boys who are to become our senators and rulers, our preachers and our teachers ; to form and lead the public sentiment, to originate the acts and the history of the nation. Is it any wonder, then, that Christianity remains only a name among us ? That in all our great opinions and practices we are as essentially Pagans as were Homer. and Thucydides themselves ? That pretending to be the disciples of the Prince of Peace, we are unblushingly the disciples, and the very zealous ones, of Mars and Bellona ?

We open Homer's Iliad, the book presented for the

study and supreme admiration of our youth, and the first words that meet us are—

" Μηνιν, ἄειδε, θεὰ Πηληϊάδεω 'Αχιλῆος
Οὐλομένην"————&c.

In fact, the gloomy wrath of Achilles, the great hero of the book which sent thousands of the brave Greeks to Hades, and occasioned unnumbered sorrows to his countrymen. The first view of this hero is in his fierce quarrel with Agamemnon ; the next in his fury for the loss of his kept mistress. Then quickly follow scenes betwixt Jove and Juno, and Paris and Helen, of a most sensuous description. We open Virgil, and it is again—" Arma virumque cano," followed by similar scenes with Æneas and Dido. Pretty reading for growing boys ! And it is not merely the reading, it is the daily and yearly study of the whole of these volumes, freighted with violence and sensuality. Where Christ says—" Love your enemies, and do good to those that hate you and despitefully use you," we say to our youth in Homer—

" 'Ω κύνες, οὔ μ' ἔτ' ἐφάσκεθ' ὑπότροπον οἴκαδ' ἱκέσθαι,
Δήμου ἀπο Τρώων,"————

" Dogs ! you have had your day ! ye feared no more
Me in the beggar from the Trojan shore."

We pronounce with Ulysses most earnestly—

" The hour of vengeance, wretches ! now is come,
Impending fate is yours, and instant doom !"

Whilst we are told that, under the influence of real Christianity, we shall beat our spears into ploughshares, and our swords into pruning-hooks, we are, as a nation, armed to the very teeth ; spending thirty or forty millions a year in warriors and war-ships.

We educate the] nations as Pagans of the highest type and deepest tone, and we expect them to become Christians. How is it possible that the meek and humane sentiments of the gospel can ever enter souls thus nurtured, thus built up ? That they can ever regard its precepts as anything but to be heard in [churches, and left there in the great church Bible, as their own proper place ? How is it to be expected that anything else should arise, when we see a nation's whole youth familiarized every day, for above ten years together— those growing, susceptible years—those years when their feelings are developing, their passions are kindling into volcanic strength — with all the rapes, and peccadilloes of gods and goddesses, whom they have learned to admire above all things, by the preference given them by the most approved of all systems of education ? We roll our children in the *Styx* of heathen grossness, and expect them, as a matter of course, to become pure as lilies and gentle as lambs. And yet is not everyone complaining of the sad tone of our public schools ? Nevertheless, so completely has custom blinded us in this respect, that the most Christian of our teachers, the most pious and sagacious of our preachers and prelates, never discern the enormity ; never suspect the rottenness of the system that they perpetuate. They put uncleanness into all the food of youth, and think that, like manure at a tree's root, it will percolate into piety, and produce most salutary fruits. "O fools and blind !" How is it that such men as Arnold and other school reformers never get a glimpse of this great Serbonian bog of moral pestilence and death ?

Yet Plato saw it, and denounced the desolating impurity of Homer and the other poets ; so that he excluded the poets altogether from his model republic. Yet the early Fathers saw it ; Lactantius saw it : and Augustine saw it. Let us look at the "Confessions" of the latter. "Over the entrance of the grammar school is a veil drawn ! True ; yet this is not so much an emblem of aught recondite as a cloak of error. Let not those whom I no longer fear, cry out against me. Let not either buyers or sellers of grammar cry out against me. But woe to thee, thou torrent of human custom. Who shall stand up against thee ? How long shalt thou remain undried up ? How long roll the sons of Eve into that huge and hideous ocean, which even they scarcely over-pass who climb the cross. Did I not read in thee of Jove the thunderer and adulterer ? * * * And now, which of our gowned masters lends a sober ear to one, who from their own school cries out : 'These were Homer's pictures — transferring things human to the gods ; would he had brought down things divine to us !' Yet more truly had he said,—' These are, indeed, his pictures, but attributing a divine nature to wicked men, that crimes might be no longer crimes, and that whoso commits them might seem to imitate not abandoned men, but the celestial gods.' And yet thou hellish torrent, into thee are cast the sons of men, with rich rewards for compassing such learning; and a great solemnity is made of it, when this is going on in the] forum, within sight of law, appointing a salary besides the scholars' payments; and thou lashest thy rocks and roarest. Hence words are learnt; hence eloquence; most necessary to gain your ends or maintain opinions. As if we should never know such words as 'golden shower,' 'lap,' 'beguile,' 'temple of the heavens,' or others in that passage, unless Terence had brought a lewd youth upon the stage, setting up Jupiter as his example of seduction. And then mark how he excites himself to lust as by celestial authority!

"'And what God? Great Jove,
Who shakes heaven's highest temples with his thunder.
And I a poor mortal man, not do the same?
I did it, and with all my heart I did it.'

"Not one whit more easily are the words learnt for all this vileness, but by their means vileness is committed with less shame. Not that I blame the words, being, as it were, choice and precious vessels, but that wine of error which is drunk to us in them by intoxicated teachers; and if we, too, drink not, we are beaten, and have no sober judge to whom we can appeal. But O, my God! in whose presence I may now without hurt remember this, all this, unhappily, I learnt willingly, with great delight, and for this was pronounced a hope-

ful boy.   Bear with me, my God, while I say something
of my wit, Thy gift, and on what dotages I was com-
pelled to waste it.   But we were forced to go astray in
the footsteps of the poetic fictions.   And was there
nothing else whereon to exercise my wit and tongue ?"

Is there nothing else, indeed, after more than a
thousand years, on which to exercise the wits and
tongues of our children ?   After all the praises of the
classic writers of antiquity, are there not to be found
sufficient prose and verse among them worthy a
Christian mind to imbibe, and a Christian memory to
retain, without the polluted pages of a Homer, or a
Virgil, or of some of their compatriots, who, with their
genius, are sources of a moral poison thus sucked in
by unsuspecting youth under the highest sanctions of
the learning, the talent, the station, and the custom of
this country ?   Are the souls of men, looking back on
their early feeding under the upas trees of classic
Greece and Rome, still to repeat the lamentations of
Augustine, and still to deplore the desolations that these
Pagan poisons have perpetrated on their lives ?   Are
men—with the gospel of peace and holiness, of a divine
purity, of a God-like forgiveness, of an arch-angelic
nobility, in their hands, daily read, or readable in their
houses, weekly read in their churches—still to have
their moral perceptions, its world-restoring truths fore-
stalled, prevented, made impossible by the Pagan vices,
diffused through every vein and artery of their bodies,
through every sense and sentiment of their souls ; and
thus to go on re-enacting old Paganism in wars and

aggressions on their neighbours for ever? Are they to scatter pollution through our cities, till men's minds stand aghast at the torrent of licentiousness that sweeps through our streets, sweeping down woman's peace and virtue to destruction, and the souls of our youth to perdition?

These are questions which it is high time for all men to ask themselves. It is not the question whether we shall learn Greek and Latin, but from what source? It is not the question whether we shall read Homer and Virgil, but when? In mature life, and with hearts and minds filled and fortified by the divine spirit and doctrine of Christianity, we may read and enjoy the nobler parts of these authors. But for God's sake, for humanity's sake, that savage war may cease to disgrace a *soi-disant* Christian world, that sensuality may be checked, discountenanced, and whipped down into its own nether regions, let not the tender minds of our children be fed on poison pregnant with death and misery, and anti-civilization, to every generation which is past, and to every generation which shall still use them.

Cast a glance over Europe. Behold its enormous armies, its despots, its raging war, its people groaning under martial taxation. Look at the enormous mass of litigation in this country, and remember the words of St. Paul, who thought it monstrous that Christians should "go to law one with another." Behold the vices of cities, and the ignorance of the poor, and ask yourselves whether this could possibly have been the Europe of to-day if a fair and manly Christianity had been taught with half the zeal and honour with which we have taught the fierce dogmas, the resentful pride, the loveless ethics, and the sensual prurience of Paganism. Augustine tells us twelve hundred years ago, that this could not have been the case in his day, " Had the tender shoots of the heart been supported by the prop of the Scriptures, so it had not trailed away amid these empty trifles, a defiled prey to the fowls of the air. For in more ways than one do we sacrifice to the rebellious angels." Augustine remarks how much more men are shocked at a barbarism of speech than of action. That they had rather hate a *human* being, than omit the aspirate in a *uman* being. That if they were pleading before a judge in public, they would feel more shame in murdering the word *human* being than in having murdered the human being himself, and this, he adds, " Was the world at whose gate unhappily I lay in my boyhood ; this the stage where I feared more to commit a barbarism, than having committed one, to envy those who had not. These things I speak and confess to Thee, my God, for which I had praise from them whom then I thought it all virtue to please."

These were professedly Pagan teachers, but would not Augustine be rather astonished if he returned to earth, after more than twelve centuries, to find a professedly Christian world still laying their children at this same gate of Pagan debauchery? But this would not be his sole astonishment. He would have more in beholding the terrible and discouraging fruits which' it has scattered over the world. Fruits more prolific of armed men than the dragons' teeth of a thousand Cadmuses or Jasons.

And yet, let no one mistake me, and say that I stamp us all as Pagans—Not so. Though I say, and that by the clearest marks and proofs of gospel test, that for any nation yet to call itself a Christian nation, is a gross assumption : yet it is equally certain that God has a large and a true Church in each. In none, perhaps, so great as in England. It is true that it is a church in the wilderness. It has grown in spite of the deep and systematic foundation of Paganism laid in education. It has grown by the labours of great and independent souls, of all sects and establishments, by such as have broken through the bondage of scholastic teachings and creeds, by such as never knew them.

By pure, diligent, unambitious men, in thousands who have borne the badge of hierarchy or anti-hierarchy on their backs, but the lamp of God's love and light in their hearts, and have gone on their way forgetting outward names and institutions in the ever-absorbing and overflowing spirit of a divine benevolence towards their fellow-men. Such men we see penetrating daily into the darkest, foulest, most man-forsaken, but not God-forsaken, purlieus .of our great cities ; undaunted by contempt, uncheered by applause, unslackened in their zeal by the prospects of an almost

boundless wickedness. God's heroes ! true, staunch
heroes ! who shall never receive estates and seats
amongst our peers for their services, but the far more
glorious heritage of those who "shine as stars in the
firmament for ever and ever." This church has grown
by the self-devotion and self-sacrifice of Catholic and
Anglo-Catholic, of assenter and dissenter, of learned
and unlearned, and it is the great cheering fact of the
age, that it is visibly and widely growing. In all ranks
and in all places, we cannot come into contact with
our fellows without discovering a deep and earnest
spirit of enquiry after a more pure and inward life.
The great cry is—

"More life and fuller 'tis we want."

Whilst the tempest of Paganism sweeps on amid
guns and drums, and the brazen music of strife and
bloodshed ; while Babylon, the harlot, still claims her
tawdry and voluptuous votaries in this wealthy and
corrupt age, there is yet "a still, small voice" of the
tender and divine whispering amongst loving hearts
and earnest, tearfully aspiring souls ; and as this
breath of the upper heavens, of the inner sanctuary of
the Saviour's peace, touches more and more of the
seeking ones as it passes, the numbers and the boun-
daries of the living undivided church must still ex-
pand. And it is to aid this expansion, to favour this
genuine life, that it is necessary that the old philosophy
of Paganism should be put into its proper place, and

the opening of life be cleared from the poison plants of Pagan passions and ideas, and be inaugurated only amid the dews and scented herbage, the flowers and free airs of unfettered, unprevented, unperverted CHRISTIANITY.

CHAPTER VI.

LUNATICS.

"Every one has his own class of madness."
Italian Proverb. See Title Page.

THE world abounds with Bedlams, where it sends
Those that it deems most mad;—oh! maddest
world!
Itself one mighty Bedlam. There it keeps
The few it deems insane.—Oh! insane world!
For these are, in the main, but harmless dreamers,
Who think themselves other than what they are,
Just as nine-tenths of those who send them there
Deem of themselves. Oh! would that none were
more
Frenzied than are the bulk of those insane ones!
Most innocent are chiefly their delusions!
Here we have one, a king, dethroned unjustly,
Yet stirring up no war for his lost crown.

And here a queen swelling with sense of state,

And fancying that her queenship is allowed;

And that her keepers are her court: so lives,

And smiles, and is most happy.

Here sits one,

A poet or poetess, lost in thoughts sublime,—

Oh ! too sublime for the prosaic tribe

'Midst whom the poet is condemned to dwell.

There walks a statesman who has saved his realm

In a most terrible crisis, and he hears

His praises sung in every chant that breaks

Through his dull walls from the blithe street beyond.

Here is a clergyman with mildest look

Who, though his village parsonage is far

Over the hills, yet hears his pleasant bells

Chime out and make his hamlet fields rejoice.

And he is in his ancient pulpit now,

And preaches to his flock with earnest zeal ;

And marks each well-known face from pew to pew.

And now, in actual deed, he takes a box,

A little wooden box from off his table,

And opens it, and lets a beetle swarm

Creep thence abroad, and counts them carefully;

And thinks they are his very congregation,

Pouring abroad, the service being done.

And there go Thomas Watson and his wife :

And Peter Buck, the keeper, and Dame Wall :

And following them the clerk, and then—himself.

And so he scoops them up, and in his box

Shuts them again till, one by one, they die.

And with grave face he reads the funeral form,

And sits him down well pleased, and is at home.

Ah ! what is this to the stupendous madness

Of real kings and ministers of state,

Who send forth men in shoals to butchery

Mutual and causeless ?   What to that of those,

The brutish mobs, who at their bidden word

Go forth like sheep in will, but tiger-like

In deadly fury howl, and curse, and hew

Each other into mangled poison heaps,

And groan and perish in their venomous gore ?

And what, if now and then a madder head

In Bedlam slyly seeks to kill his warder,

Or fellow lunatic ?   How mild a madness

To that of those who kill their hecatombs.

To that of those who march as they are led

To murder men whom they have never known,

And, therefore, could not wrong them.   Fathers and
      sons

And brothers, loved of sad, dependent souls,

Who by their fall, have fallen to life-long woe !

NOTE TO CHAPTER VI.

IT is a hopeful sign that writers for the daily press are beginning to recognise the utter insanity of the war-spirit which has seized upon Europe.

The correspondent of the *Daily Telegraph* writing from Paris, Nov. 30th, and describing the horrors occurring around that doomed city, very wisely observes of the inhabitants of a celebrated mad-house in the suburbs of Paris : " The mad inhabitants are about the most sane people I have heard of in these parts. They enjoy good health—barring their antics—they stay within doors, and allow those, who are supposed to be in the enjoyment of their senses, to be wounded and killed in thousands."

CHAPTER VII.

NO CHRISTIAN NATIONS.

WE talk of CHRISTIAN NATIONS. 'Tis a vile
And rank abuse of words : for there are none,
Nor ever were. There never can be such
Who fight and murder. 'Tis a contradiction
Of terms and things : of sense and sentiment.

    Look at your gospels : read them as they stand.
Blench not and quibble not at what you see ;
And ye shall find no possible escape
From the broad fact—that fighting nations still
Are pagan, and insult the name of Christ.
    THERE ARE NO CHRISTIAN NATIONS; NEVER
        WERE.
Christ ratified the old command of God—
" Thou shalt not kill." And he went far beyond

5

In his own teaching.   " Thou shalt not resist
Even, evil.   If struck, strike not again,
But to the smiter turn thy other cheek.
And render good for evil; for curses, blessing.
Thou shalt not *kill* thine enemy, but love him,
And do him good ; in this thy Heavenly Father
Following, who doth send his sun and rain
On evil and good alike."

                  These are his words.
And wilt thou call them metaphorical,
Not meant to be enacted to the letter ?
I tell thee, nay.   For Christ did demonstrate
Their strict, inevitable import; did himself
Carry them out, and wrote them in his blood.

    Beaten, insulted, spit upon, O man !
In thy own pagan leaven, in thy old
Notions of noble spirit and of honour,
Thou wouldst have struck again, revenged, and died.

    Beaten, insulted, spit upon and killed,
The Son of Heaven revealed a loftier phase
Of courage, a far nobler class of mind
Than lie within thy nature.   He stood forth

The perfect image of godlike fortitude ;
Struck not, reviled not, but put forth unmoved
A matchless bravery, a suffering strength,
Before which all the pagan vaunts of glory,
And martial magnanimity, and fame
Sink into meanness.   Yours is but the old
Dogma of Jewish vengeance ; that of eye
For eye, tooth for tooth,—the savage law
Of brute retaliation.   That of Christ
Whom ye pretend to serve, is self cast down,
And heaven upon its ruins raised in power ;
Victorious over every mortal circumstance :
Over all force, and time, and death itself.

Christ from the bitter cross looked calmly down,
And praying for his ruthless murderers, said,
" Father forgive, they know not what they do !"
There you have word and deed, the law and act
Of your professed example—of your God !
And those who act not thus are none of his.
And would ye know whence wars and fightings
   come ? *

* James, General Epistle, iv., 1, 2, 3.

What makes a Prussian Wilhelm, or a Bismark?

Ye have their origin in the eloquent words

Of one of Christ's elect ambassadors—

"From whence come wars and fightings? Come
  they not

From your own lusts, that in your members war?

Ye lust and have not; kill and desire to have.

Ye fight and war, yet have not, for ye seek

But to consume your substance on your lusts."

  These are the servant's words,—what says the
    Lord?

"Ye seek to kill me, for my living word *

No place has in you : ye are of your Father

The Devil, and ye will surely do his lusts—

A liar, and a murderer from the first."

  Away then with the name of CHRISTIAN
    NATIONS:

Whom Christ condemns, and utterly disowns.

The fighters have no right nor part in him,

But he has fixed their parentage elsewhere—

Sons of the Devil, "that Murderer from the first."

   * Gospel of St. John, viii., 37—44.

And when hereafter they shall cry to him,
" Lord ! Lord !" then will he answer them and say,
" Depart ye wicked, for I never knew you."

Yet, though these warring nations are not Christ's,
Still he has in them many, many children.
Living his life, and praying to be his,
And loving as he loved, and these he owns—
His suffering seed, the children of his Cross,
Who live like Lot in Sodom, and suspend
The uplifted arm of God's fierce visitation.
They are the salt that keep these blood-stained
      peoples
From foul decay, else had their doom long since
Sunk them to dust, like battling realms of old.

But ye have learned the logic of the school
That is beneath ; the trite old sophistry,
The last resource of the hard-driven man,
Defender of the hydra curse of earth—
" Ah ! were but all states Christian ! gladly then
We'd sheathe the sword and hush the noisy drum."
No doubt ; but wherein then would be your merit ?
What ! has it cost so much from age to age,

In wealth, and national woes, and lives of men,
To follow up the bloody track of death,
And shall it cost you nothing to fix Peace
On an eternal basis ?   Nothing to make
Your Christian creed and practices agree ?
Nothing to make you, in the eye of God,
What you so long have claimed to be, and are not ?
Nothing to grasp the teachings of our Lord
In a profounder and more real sense,
As words of living force and truths of heaven ?

But, say the world-wise reasoners, unsubdued,
" Think ye that we shall sit like sheep, and let
Some horde of human butchers cut our throats ?
And seize our country, and our happy homes ;
And revel in our wealth, and own our lands ;
And strike no blow ?   That were the act of fools !"

So ! ye are wiser than your sovereign prince,
Whose name ye blazon on your spiritual banners !
Why, 'tis the very thing your captain did l .

Our Lord proclaimed an everlasting Peace,
A peace the fruit of love ; a peace which none
Should ever, on subtlest plea, or gravest cause,

Dare to infringe ; a peace in which no man

Should raise an arméd hand against another.

Should never more, like the fierce tribes of old,

Deface, much less destroy, the temple of God,

Man's body, in which he dwells in mystic life,

With the hushed soul, his offspring. And this law,

Which was the law of heaven now brought to earth,

Having decreed, he sealed it with his blood.

 That which he claimed from man, its mainten-

  ance,

As sacred and inviolable, he himself

Scorned to infract : but, knowing death the fine

For its observance, with a steadfast heart

He met it, and in that great act bequeathed

His purpose and example to all time.

 And think'st thou, man, that thou can'st follow

  Christ

And not partake his sufferings ?   Can'st follow

And yet not follow him ?   Can'st tread his path

With half a heart, and less than half a faith ?

Oh ! vain endeavour !   Vain and futile hope !

For he has said, " Thou can'st not serve two mas-

  ters."

Thou can'st not serve him and the world ; nor be
At peace with him and with mankind at war.

   No plea of country, patriotism, or right ;
No law of creed, or state, or law of custom ;
No fear of punishment, or finger of scorn ;
No menaced evil of whatever kind
Can touch the great command—" Thou shalt not
     kill."

   Christ has proclaimed aloud, and down the track
Of time his voice comes sounding ever more
" Whoever seeks to save his life shall lose it ;
Who loses his for my sake, shall not die."

   Oh ! wise and learned world, thy wisdom
Is but rank foolishness with God, all-wise.
There's a philosophy more sure than thine,—
·The wisdom of a perfect faith in God,—
Reliance full and gladsome as the child's
In the fond mother's heart.   But thou, wise world,
With all thy boasts, dost never trust in God.
Broadly and clearly in the gospel page
Stands our Lord's pledge—" Whoever trusts in me
Shall never be forsaken."   It is there—

Yet in thy talk of war, thou still dost hold

That wars must be, and thou must fight and slay

When wicked men invade.   Still art thou prompt

To contradict God to his face, and treat

As folly supreme, a law divine which yet

NEVER BY ANY NATION HAS BEEN TRIED.

Search thou all history, tell me where and when

A nation standing firm on Christ's command

War to renounce, in honour of his law,

Has been by other nations over-run ?

For such a fact thy search shall be in vain.

First test the promises of God : prove first

Whether his sacred word has in it life,

And truth substantial.   Try, and if it fail

Then thou can'st speak upon a national base,

Can'st boldly stand and say " My word is fact."

But until this be done thy word is nought.

And yet this charter of earth's surest peace,

This promise of the Highest *has* been tried

By holy men who did not doubt of God.

CHAPTER VIII.

GEORGE FOX.

OH ! simple-hearted, lion-hearted Fox !
Thou hadst no weak distrust of Him who built
The heavens and earth, and their unfailing laws
Based on his word alone.   Who by his will
Holds the vast universe in fixity,
And still, from age to age, throughout all space
Wheeleth the ponderous spheres on nothing poised
But on his thought, that—thus it is and shall be !
   Sorrowing at heart, and grievously perplexed,
Fox, young, noble in mind, and seeking truth,
Saw the black, ghastly cleft between the world
And its professions : Christ upon its creed, .
Confusion in its heart ; and all the woes
And wickedness that welled from this foul source ;

And sought from men set up as Christian lights
And gospel guides, for convoy through this chaos,
And found none.   So to woods and wilds
He took his way, the Bible in his hand,
And there through days and nights, and driving
     storms
With prayers unutterable in human speech,
With groans and bitter tears, he called on Him
Who gave this lore to open its true sense.
And, as of old in Horeb's desert cave
The dauntless prophet who had firmly stood
With iron will and faith invincible,
When all around had fallen away to Baal,
And had done deeds of strange astonishment
In honour of God, and in his present power ;
But now lone, prostrate and forsaken lay
And prayed to die.   And as to him there came,
After fierce winds and earthquakes, the still·voice
Whose gentleness is life : so now to Fox
Came the full light from God, that his Son's law
Was love, and, therefore, could not be in league
With strife, or passion, or revenge of men,

But was a law of suffering, and through it
The root of conquest over secular strength.

  So, in this high conviction he went forth
To preach this gospel wisdom through the world.
It was a desperate world! The bigot state
Sensual and tyrannous, and the bigot church,—
The nation's, not the Saviour's church,—a thing
Born of man's will and laws, and not of God's,
Though claiming to be Christ's. These hand in
     hand
Forcing men's consciences, made deadly work
Throughout the land, and sowed wild violence,
Like the black dust of Egypt, in its plagues.

  Their doings were not any angels' doings,
Nor those of men who knew the gospel truth,
But such as the worst fiends from the worst nooks
Of Satan's kingdom would have revelled in.
No man should think but what the rulers thought;
No man believe but what the church believed;
The gospel was in print but not in power.
The British Inquisition in full strength,
But bearing other name, crushed England down.

The pride-inflated bishops sate and sent

The lowest ruffians of the land to drag

The conscientious pastor from his flock

And from his happy home; and bent he not,

And sold his conscience for a hollow peace,

Severed him from his fold, and thrust him down

Into some hideous dungeon, there to rot.

So Fox with his bold cry of gospel truth

Found himself quickly in a terrible storm

Raging in maddest fury from all winds.

Insensate mobs, led on by magistrates,

And bitter priests, beat him and threw him forth

Into the streets and lanes with deadly wrath;

Left him for dead, and finding him alive,

Hauled him to prison. There for many a year,

From time to time, he lay and suffered all

That cruel men could scheme of cruelty.

And dreadful were the dungeons of those days,

Vile as the men who kept them in their midst.

Dens of the direst filth, vermin and cold;

The rotten roofs open to drenching rains;

The walls around poisonous with dripping slime;

The fetid air deadly with crippling frost.

And many were the gentle friends of Fox,

Women, and tender children, and old men,

Who perished in those hells for conscience sake.

But none of these could kill or conquer Fox.

Even from his dungeon he proclaimed God's truth,

And when by intervals, he came abroad,

He marched at once to parliament and prince,

And like the fearless prophets of the past,

He bade them stand, and tremble, and reform.

Till by the power of truth he had compelled

The worldly dignities to bow to right.

Forced them to yield him liberty, and forced

Them likewise by determinate form of law

To free his people from the deadly crime

And black responsibility of war.

Oh ! triumph of pure mind, most nobly won !

Blazon eternal of the power of faith ;

Glory eternal of the Sons of Peace !

CHAPTER IX.

PENN AND PENNSYLVANIA.

AND now, at length, thou holy Oracle,—
Spirit of Truth, whom earth cannot receive,
Because it seeth not nor knoweth Thee ;*
Thou Lord of Heaven, and heaven-inspired song
Hast now vouchsafed a proof of thine own truth,
The evidence of thy inviolate word,
Which faileth not, and shall not fail, even when
The skies, and earth, and ocean fleet away.

    Forth at this juncture came the fitting man.
The follower of Fox, illustrious Penn,
Baptized with the same spirit ; illumed of God
And armed in meekness to the needful pitch
Of daring and endurance, took his place

* Gospel of St. John, xiv. 6.

And put the charter of Christ to fullest proof.

    Penn, of a warrior race, endowed with wealth,
And with the culture of the highest schools,
And walking in the sunshine and the strength
Of royal favour; with a genius framed
For high diplomacy and work of state,
And thus with mortal glory's pathways open
To his ambition, with sublimer light
Surrounded and transpierced, renounced such aims.
Like the great law-giver of the Hebrew race,
He scorned the pleasures of sin for a brief season,
And joined himself to the oppressed and low:
And through this abnegation of all self
Rose into purer greatness, and became
The founder of a state and a state's law
Nobler than this world's wise ones ever planned.

    The England of Penn's days was a harsh land.
It bore the name of Christian, but the fruits
Of bitter bigotry. Crime stalked abroad
Costumed like piety; disorder, misnamed order,
Rode roughshod over every sacred right;
And liberty of thought, and speech, and pen

Was branded, pilloried; and force enthroned
Put out God's light in the high name of God.

And yet the iron myrmidons of state
Were Christian all, forsooth, and did their deeds
Of fiendish cruelty in the holiest name !

The worship of the friends of peace and love
Was broken in upon by savage crews
Of drunken troopers, and their sanctuaries
Were rent and tumbled into heaps of ruins.
The worshippers themselves were dragged to jails,
Foul Pandemoniums of the vilest vice ;
And their goods seized, and auctioned to the mob.
Penn and his chiefest friends had no exemption.
They lay in odious dens for months or years,
And only were brought thence to be adjudged
In courts which knew no justice, and by men
Who sate in insolence of office,—stormed,
Brow-beat, and railed at them as felons base.

Yet nobly did they stand, all unabashed
And with brave souls, and calm, unblenching brow,
Did stoutest battle for their country's laws :

6

And raised their voice for liberty and right,
And won them too, and left them unto us !
　But now woke other thoughts.　For God has said
He cannot always strive with stubborn man ;
Nor yet can men strive ever with each other.
The strain upon the most enduring spirit
In constant wrestle with an evil race
Wears it like wasting poison.　The strong heart,
Armed still to fight, concessionless as steel,
Yet yearns for peace, though 'twere in some wild
　　place,
Freed from the fret and goad of wickedness.
　So Penn gazed round for refuge from the storm
Of malice most unchristian, Christian named,
And saw the magic needle of life's bark
The compass of the Spirit, ever true,
Veer, and stand fixed towards the distant West.
Then over him came streaming wondrous thoughts.
The memory of that great Occident,
That continent of continents, which God
Through unsuspecting ages kept concealed
Within the veil of his broad Providence,

Till the fit time ; and till that time had given
In heritage to the red Indian race.

A glorious land it was, colossal, vast,
A home for nations, an unstinted field
For states on states, and families and tribes,
Pouring in eager haste from crowded realms,
To freedom and large room for generations.
It was a world of rivers and woods immense,
Mountains, and plains, and valleys, that could take
Millions on millions to its mother bosom,
And feed and nourish to exuberant life,
And yet say, "Come ! my heart has room for more !"

True, that wild race, its then inhabitants,
Were of repute most evil. Those who sought
Abode amongst them, painted them as fiends.
Cruel, vindictive, treacherous, and base,
Tearing from their war-victims the red scalps ;
Torturing them like skilled Inquisitors ;
And one historian has gone so far
As to declare them children of the devil ;
That were his pen the quill of porcupine,
And his ink aquafortis, they must fail

To show them the black monsters that they were.*

And much of this was true, too true, but then

, These same self-lauding Christian visitants

Had been to them the savagest of guests.

Had landed on their coasts with banner and brand,

Self-named apostles of the Prince of Peace,

But bearing war and rapine in their belts.

Seizing their lands; burning their huts, and chasing

Their wives and children to the woods.   In change

For offered friendship, raining leaden death,

From blunderbuss and gun; and with their swords

Scoring upon their heads their lordship stern;

Stealing by night upon their sleeping bands,

They dealt them wholesale murder in wild joy;

And by such deeds they taught the law of Christ,

And marvelled that they won no proselytes;

But what they won was that which they desired

The rich demesnes of these wild warriors.

And these poor sons of nature, quick to feel,

And having in them, with all human kind,

The taint of madness from the nether spheres,—

* Cotton Mather, in his History of New England.

Rose rioting in blood, and made their foes

Tremble at the dread war-whoop from the woods,

In dark, wild nights, in lonely homes afar.

And yet these warriors deadly and terrible,

Had better nature in them. They had come

Travelling in old times from the East, and brought

Traditions of God and angels, and their walk

And talk sublime, and counsels with their fathers.

And they had minds clear-visioned,—far beyond

The brutish worship of material forms;

Knew the Great Spirit, owned his inward law,

And listened to his voice in the dim depths

Of their vast woods; and caught prophetic gleams.

Of coming things; and had a large fore-knowledge

Of the pale-faces sailing from the East,

In their huge war-canoes, the hosts of death

To the red man, with all his race and name.

But of these hunters Penn had little dread.

With all their vices they had natural hearts.

They still were undebauched by venomous creeds .

Distilled by wily priests. Their mental strength

Remained unsapped; their faculties undimmed

By metaphysic philtres charged with death,

In the laboratories of the church,

To blind the simple and to slay the wise.

Their spiritual constitutions were intact,

And all their faculties and senses sound

Save for the madness common to mankind.

And Penn preferred immensely, and with right,

A real savage to a pseudo saint.

So forth he sailed with his devoted troop

Of kindred-hearted friends, and made the coast

Of the New World near the broad Schuylkyll's banks;

And sent a proclamation through the woods

Far round, that Men of Peace were come, and
      sought

To make their dwelling with the hunter tribes.

That they were worshippers and sons like them

Of the Great Spirit, and, therefore, brothers true.

That they renounced all arms, all war, all strife,

And sought alone, on duly-purchased lands,

A home with them of rest and mutual love.

Great was the wonder in the wigwams caused

By this strange message, strange to red men's ears.

For those so-called good Christians, had been wont
To treat with them by arquebus and sword.
With blood-hounds to pursue them through the
    swamps,
And take their lands by craft and violence.

   Their first, quick impulse was to flee away
Into their farthest wilds ; but the red heralds
Appeased them by reports of these new guests ;
And they resolved to go and judge once more
Of these pale-faces, but to go all armed
And in their fullest numbers.   So they came.

   It was a sight, as from their shadowy woods
These warriors with their war-paint, spears and
    bows,
And tomahawks, and shaven and plumed heads,
Came streaming, throng on throng, and gathered
    close
A ghastly circle, round a simple knot
Of men in simplest guise,—it was a sight
To make the world's wise people inly tremble
And look for certain death.   But Penn stood calm,
And pointed to the lands which he would buy,

And to the bales of merchandise for payment :
And by the interpreter explained his wish
To purchase a large tract, where he and his
Might build their town, and cultivate their fields :
And in his hand he held a written Treaty
Which the contracting parties in true love
Bound, in true amity to live together,
While sun and moon endured.

     And unto this
The chiefs and sages of the woods assented,
Gladly and cordially, and pledged their faith
And smoked the pipe of peace : and in pure trust
Carried the written pledge of Father Onas,
For so they now named Penn, and all their goods
Back to their hunting-grounds, in wonder and joy.
And thus, in Voltaire's words, was promptly framed
" THE ONLY TREATY MADE WITHOUT AN OATH,
THE ONLY ONE THAT NEVER HAS BEEN BROKEN !"

 Great triumph of the faith and truth of Christ !
Great monument of War's most needless curse !
Standing alone amid the blood-stained ages,
How is it that men will not look at thee ?—

How is it that they still persist in killing
With such clear proof of practicable peace?
  These savage, violent, and lawless men,
As painted by the men termed civilized,
Yet felt and honoured truth.   Trusted, they trusted,
And when in future years fierce wars sprang up
Betwixt the colonies and mother land,
And they were feed and tempted by these foes
To add their horrors to the bloody strife,
They still remembered Father Onas ; still
Preserved their pledge to him inviolate.
And whilst they dealt their fury, round and round,
In daily wastings, or in nightly raids,
They never, with their knowledge, touched a hair
Of any head that held the creed of Penn.

CHAPTER X

MODERN WARFARE.

AH ! if men *would* be Christians ! Would become
After such awful ages what they fain
Would have us think them ! If they would assume
The fact as well as name and fame of Christians.
If they would try the policy of Penn,
In preference to the policy of kings,
What a most wondrous era for mankind !

  If kings and ministers of state would labour
A thousandth part as much to foster Peace,
As they do to make war. If they would spend
A hundred millionth part of the vast wealth
That they have spent on war, in checking war.
If they had been as zealous to avoid
Subject of discord and the guilt of blood,

As they have been to challenge, rob and slay.

If people styling themselves pious and wise,

Had forced their governments, as was their duty,

To pick no quarrels, wound no neighbour state ;

In spleen 'gainst kings, lay waste with murderous
    troops

No lands of innocent peasants ; if the priests,

Naming themselves as Christ's, had dared to preach

The very words of Christ.   If learned scribes

Had not in fine and milk-and-water phrase,

Said war was bad, and peace was very good—

But in the tone of bold and genuine wisdom,

Had branded war as treason unto God,

And devil-work by gospel law condemned.

Had gentle woman, oracle of home,*

The priestess of the heart, the fashioner

Of all men in soft childhood's plastic years,

And youth's unfolding ; had she, unseduced

By fictions of the hells, by talk of glory,

Which is the glory only of the realms

Of nethermost strife and malice :—

Unseduced by pleas of patriotism

* See note, p. 98.

And lust of social honour, had she taught
That the true bravery is to curb our wills ;
That truest honour lies in love of neighbour ;
That truest wisdom lies in force of reason,
And eloquence of purpose to smooth out
Causes of difference ; and religion's work
To reconcile, and pacify and bless ;
That mutual slaughter is the act of fools,
And they who practise it are mad, or worse,
And should be stamped with the world's infamy.

In one brief word, had there been Christian nations,
Not names alone ; and man, indeed, been bent
To do Christ's will, and bear the cross he bore,
Love unto death, and death unto themselves
Rather than murder,—war had long ago
Become a ghastly legend like the tale
Of cannibal orgies in dark lands abhorred.

But we are not so blest in all our pride
Of knowledge and virtue.   The old madness still
Is terrible in our blood ; and hence we stand
Nation in face of nation, highly Christian
Yet most intent on murder.   Hosts immense

Are held in every land termed civilised
Ready for instant slaughter, ready armed
With instruments of death and desolation
Such as the pagan nations never knew. ·
Tools and machines of a capacity for crime
And massacre stupendous and infernal,
A million-deviled power. A power that art,
And chemic science, and the giant strengths
Of fire and steam, intended for the good
And ornament of life, but seized by death,
And wielded by the maniac rage of man,
Is driven forth to lay whole kingdoms waste ;
To knock down cities, and destroy all works
Of beauty and of pleasance ; to sweep files
Of human creatures at one blast from life
As so much worthless carrion. So we stand.

But this is little. These vast hosts of carnage
Are but a fragment of our monstrous life.
Now every man is disciplined to war ;
And at the call of some fanatic king,*
Starts up at once, and grimly stands enmassed,
Shoulder to shoulder, one vast merciless horde,

* See note, p. 99.

A body mechanised to organic power,
Moving with the same prompt and accurate skill,
The same remorseless stress as hammer and wheel,
As crank and cylinder, beneath one will.

  And at this will forth stalks this Frankenstein,
With all its myriad feet to trample down
A nation at its tread : with its vast mouth
To eat a nation's substance as it goes ;
With all its myriad hands to snatch and seize,
To kill, and rend to fragments all its goods.
So as it moves, the ground is gory mud :
The mangled bodies of men its stepping-stones ;
Around it hell's fierce tempest, and behind
A land, not of the shadow of death, but death itself.

  So at this instant tramp the German hordes,
Like to their Teutsch and Vandal sires of old,
One total, martially compacted nation,
Seven hundred thousand men with swarms behind
From every nook remote of Fatherland :
And on they go with all their steeds and trains
Of ponderous artillery and piled munitions.
Even the Steam Plough, wrested from its labours,—

Reversing dreadfully the Prophet's promise

Of sheathéd swords being beaten into ploughshares—

Is pressed into the hideous war of kings ;

And snorting, drags over the groaning acres,

Of trampled corn, and vine-lands, murderous

    cannon.

  And Wilhelm, their pious king, rides at their head,

And hourly calls on God for further mercies *

Of bleeding hecatombs.   On his own God

He calls,—not upon our God—but on Moloch !

  And on before him run his proclamations :—

" Good people, sit ye still ; make no resistance ;

And on our royal faith, we will not hurt you.

Your lives, your goods, your trade shall be respected :

Only sit still, and let us peel you well !"

  And the right royal son of royal Wilhelm,

Riding so mildly at his army's head,

Sends proclamation second.—" People of France !

---

  * See the telegrams of King Wilhelm to his Queen from
the seat of war.   The lines of the poem are almost literal
transcripts of these telegrams.   After the most bloody actions
he says,—" May God grant us more of these mercies !"   See
also the proclamation of the Crown Prince of Prussia.

Our war is not with you, but with Napoleon !"
So on he rides, and yet the People of France
Find at his hands war in its vilest shape,
War undeclared—if we can read him right—
Which is the worst of wars when it is made.

  So on they go, Father and Son, so pious,
Humane, and truthful ! They have now the monarch
On whom alone they war. Yet turn they back ?
Do they cry halt to their devouring legions ?
Do they restrain their hands from peasant spoils ?
Do they desist from their fierce sack of cities ?
    Let Strasburg, Toul, and Metz and Phalsburg
      speak !
Proclaim their deeds of justice, thou sad cry
Of babes and women bursting in appeal
From out the flaming church ! Speak, oh ! thou
      wail
Of agony, sweeping through the silent night
In mournful cadence from grim ambulances,
Making the heart of men stand still with awe !
Proclaim their deeds of mercy, ye pale prisoners,
Famished and crouched in pestilential slime,

Midst heaps of slaughtered steeds, livid and foul!

Proclaim their love, thou heroine of Bazeilles,

Thou metamorphosed tigress—once a woman—

A wife, a mother! Bereft of all but hate—

Thou piteous type of thy great land's despair,

As with thy frenzied, Amazonian arm

Thou in mad fury "to the bitter end"

Dost fight and die! Proclaim their chivalry

Thou aged, heart-sick man, Alsatian father,

Who didst, to hide thy girls from war's fierce lust,

Immure them, like pale nuns in days of old,

Not for the sake of their lost innocence,

But to preserve them pure,—heaping in love

Around them store of food for many days!

Proclaim their truth, thou aged, weeping woman,

Proclaim their pity with thy dolorous plaint—

" They have left us but our eyes to weep our woe !"

NOTES TO CHAPTER X.

Note, page 91, line 14—

Had gentle woman, oracle of home.

" The child
Ere he can lisp his mother's sacred name,
Swells with the unnatural pride of crime, and lifts
His baby sword even in a hero's mood.
This infant-arm becomes the bloodiest scourge
Of devastated earth ; whilst specious names,
Learnt in soft childhood's unsuspecting hour,
Serve as the sophisms with which manhood dims
Bright reason's ray, and sanctifies the sword ⸱ ,
Upraised to shed a brother's innocent blood.".

SHELLEY.

" Men by their nature are prone to fight ; they will
fight for any cause or for none. . . . . Men can bear
the sight of suffering, injustice, misery in the earth,
but you (women) should not be able to bear the sight
of it. Men may tread it down without sympathy in
their own struggle ; but men are feeble in sympathy
and contracted in hopes ; it is you only who can feel

the depths of pain, and conceive the way of its heal-
ing. Instead of trying to do this you turn away from
it."

RUSKIN'S " SESAME AND LILIES."

———

Note, page 93, line 20—

And at the call of some fanatic king.

" I have no words for the wonder with which I hear
Kinghood still spoken of, even among thoughtful men,
as if governed nations were a personal property, and
might be bought and sold, or otherwise acquired, as
sheep, of whose flesh their King was to feed, and whose
fleece he was to gather ; as if Achilles' indignant
epithet of base kings ' people-eating ' were the constant
and proper title of all monarchs ; and enlargement of
a king's dominion meant the same thing as the in-
crease of a private man's estate.   Kings who think so,
however powerful, can no more be the true kings of a
nation than gad-flies are the kings of a horse ; they
suck it, and may drive it wild, but do not guide it."

RUSKIN.

———

The Prussians and their German allies have missed
a great glory.   Had they, when they had taken the
French Emperor prisoner, and captured the army of
MacMahon, in accordance with the proclamation of

7—2

the Crown Prince, ceased their operations, and declared
that notwithstanding the threatened invasion of Ger-
many, they had no wish to inflict the calamities of war
on the French people, they would, by so noble a mag-
nanimity, have won the applause of the whole world ;
left a grateful feeling in the hearts of the French nation,
and won more solid advantages than they ever can, by
ruthlessly trampling down a whole country in the eyes
of indignant Europe.

But they who were acquainted with the real charac-
ter of the Prussians, could have no such expectations.
That character is destitute of a generous magnanimity ;
is savage, overbearing, insolent, and bent on the utmost
revenge ; and with this character they have succeeded
in thoroughly inoculating their formerly good-natured
neighbours, the Germans.

The Prussian system of arming and thoroughly
disciplining a whole male population, has now revealed
in the heart of Europe a most frightful phenomenon.
Such a system, that of marching out *en masse*, and
bearing down a whole nation by overwhelming num-
bers, once inaugurated, as it now has been, must
become the system of all Europe. No nation is any
longer safe, when 700,000 men march down on a
country, with a reserve of 800,000 more, according to
the statements of the Germans themselves. All must
adopt the same system. Already Russia is, and has
been for some time, preparing armaments on a gigantic
scale. France fallen, Turkey once more seems within
her grasp. The manufacturers of England, Belgium,

and America cannot supply arms and machines of war fast enough for her. From that quarter fresh displays of bloody operations on a tremendous scale are inevitable.

This Prussian system of warfare, notwithstanding the bravery of any troops concerned, is essentially a cowardly system—a system of enormously developed brute force ! It consists, not merely in the perfection of discipline, but in bearing its enemies down by over-whelming numbers. It is a system destitute of all sense of honour or fair-play. As a friend has well observed : " Napoleonism in France, and Frederickism at Berlin, are identically the same principle, that of a ruffianly passion for war and aggression, and of a total disregard of the peace and rights of your neigh-bour." There can be no more palpable truth. The Prussian system is at the same time as utterly con-temptuous of faith and of the most solemn engage-ments as it is callous to human suffering. And this has always been the case. Wolfgang Menzel, in his History of Germany, describes the perfidious charac-ter of the so-called Great Frederick in indignant colours. He says that in his war with Maria Theresa of Austria, he made with her an engagement to sus-pend operations from a certain day in winter to a certain day in spring, but that the moment the Em-press, in unsuspecting faith, withdrew her troops, he rushed in, and seized one of her provinces ! Our own historians have to complain of similar acts of perfidy from Prussia. They state that in our early operations against the French Republic, Prussia had engaged to join us in Belgium to drive the French thence. On being reminded that it was time to march to the place of rendezvous, the King of Prussia sent word that it was impossible to move his army without money. In consequence a remittance of £2,000,000 was made, whereupon he marched indeed, but it was to join Russia and Austria in the seizure and division of Poland! so that our English money was made the means of that most infamous transaction, and our troops in Belgium were caused great loss and suffering by the non-appearance of the Prussian allies. By the 5th article of the Treaty of ·Prague, Prussia bound herself to restore North Schleswick to Denmark, but she has steadily ignored the fact, though constantly reminded of it by Denmark.

Entirely in keeping with this conduct has been the Prussian contempt of their own proclamations during this French campaign. From the day on which Napoleon and his army were captured, the Germans had no business in France, and though some English journals have endeavoured to defend this flagrant breach of faith, foreign ones, and the people in all countries, have cried eternal shame upon it.

The manner in which the King of Prussia has kept the words of his own proclamation that the people of France should not be hurt in their lives, trade, or property, where they made no resistance, has no parallel in history in its most barbarous infamy. Everywhere, whether the people resisted or not, the correspondents of our own newspapers have shown in the most ample details, that the whole country of France, where the German armies advanced, was stripped of every possible article of food, and left a trampled desert. · This was, however, but a repetition of 1814, when of all the allied armies marching on Paris, that of Prussia left a track across France of ruin, never forgotten.

The same utter callousness of nature has marked frequently their treatment of their prisoners in the present war, seemingly forgetful that a soldier may become a prisoner himself. An eye-witness (an Englishman), writing from Sedan to the *Daily Telegraph*, says, " After MacMahon's army surrendered as prisoners of war, in a plot of meadow ground, not damp, but positively soaking wet, about as large as Trafalgar Square, 80,000 men were huddled together like sheep. Of these about 20,000 were soon marched off to Germany, and whilst I was present 10,000 men and about 300 officers were started on their way to the railway, which will take them into Prussia. But I visited them before they left, and a more deplorable scene it would be impossible to imagine. Not one ounce of meat had been served to them, and all they had to live upon was one hard biscuit per man for every two days. The Prussian authorities would not allow their prisoners even to purchase what they required. As for the men, they were, if possible, in a more deplorable state than the officers. Many were flushed with raging fever : others were suffering from all the different phases of severe bowel complaint, and hundreds could barely stand upright from rheumatic pains, but no doctor had been near them. They were marched off, preceded by a military band playing triumphant Prussian airs, were made to march in sections as if on parade, and even the French officers, if they lagged behind for an instant, were beaten with the butt-ends of muskets, and roared at, 'Forwards, forwards.' Weak, sick, and more than half starved as they were, and suffering from dysentery, fever, wet clothes, and rheumatism, these men—officers and soldiers alike—were hurried along the road for a march of ten miles at a pace very nearly equal to our double quick time in English marching."

There wanted only one atrocity to render the Prussian invasion of France for ever infamous in history, and this was found in the new military law promulgated by the Prussian authorities, that all persons, men or women, who dared to defend their country against the invaders, without having on a regular soldier's uniform, on being taken, should be treated as outlaws and vagabonds, and hanged or shot at once. Patriotism in all times has been regarded as one of the noblest of virtues, and Tell and Hofer have been celebrated enthusiastically in German songs, and Tell especially by the illustrious Schiller, but the Prussians would have shot both Tell and Hofer, had they lived now, and been taken in this war, as lawless villains. It is a fine specimen of Prussian arrogance, the charging French peasantry with *treason* against Germany, in assuming to defend themselves against foreign marauders.

Wherever any resistance by the population has been made the place has at once been burnt to the ground by the German commanders, often with a majority of the inhabitants within it. The fate of Bazeilles, Bazan, Ablis, and other towns, has justly excited the indignation of Europe.

Amid the unmanly treatment of women in carrying out this Prussian system, facts occurred of the most incredible nature. One of these is very characteristic. According to an account from a private letter published in London, and widely circulated in the newspapers, a young woman in a village near Strasburg, who had been violated and most grossly used by a Prussian soldier, seized a hatchet and cut off two of his fingers. For this she was dragged before the commanding officer. In Wellington's army the man would have hanged on the next tree, but in the Prussian,'the woman was at once hanged for avenging the outrage on her person !

The *Daily Telegraph* of Oct. 14 says, "The news is brought from the head-quarters of King William himself that the town of Ablis had been burnt down because a squadron of Hussars had been suddenly attacked in the night *through the treachery of the inhabitants;* another instance of the innocent punished with the guilty, if indeed Frenchmen are 'guilty' when aiding their own troops. Again, we have the statement announced with cold-blooded precision, as if the fact were matter of boast, that, up to Tuesday last 'about twenty villages had been burnt,' and 150 peasants, including 'women and children,' shot, for carrying on what Count Bismark's journalists term 'illicit' warfare against Germany. Last of all, we find Count Bismark coolly calculating that the siege of Paris, in which he persists, in order to secure Alsace and Lorraine, will cause hundreds of thousands to die of starvation."

But what is the whole of this most unchristian campaign but a detail of the most persevering persistence in unnecessary bloodshed, and in the perpetration of the most unmanly and disgraceful deeds ? Whole villages burnt down with the women and children in the cellars : women with their hands tied behind them, brought out to be shot for assisting their husbands and brothers in defence of their invaded country. The maddened woman of Bazeilles who attempted to revenge the slaughter of her husband and sons shot. Fathers building up their daughters within walls with a store of provisions to save them from the lust of the Prussian soldiers. The whole of the wine presses and vats of the peasantry made useless by the German troopers having filled them with horse-dung and all manner of filth : and the whole country left without an atom of food to certain famine and death. Bismark himself calculating that not mere hundreds of thousands, but that 500,000 at least of the French people would thus perish of famine ! Women shot by order of the German commanders for resisting the violation of their persons, as published in the London newspapers. In fact, the details of the English correspondents on the battle-fields of such horrors and dastardly crimes would fill many large volumes. They will remain to stamp the conduct of the Prussians and their Prussianised allies as the most infamous in history. And yet, in the published orders of Frederick William III. of Prussia to the Landwehr in 1813, he earnestly recommends every man who could get a gun to shoot down the French from behind hedge or tree, or the walls of houses, on every possible occasion !

The Barclay brewers, who severely chastised the Austrian general, Haynau, on his visit to London, for his ordering the flogging of women in the Hungarian revolt, what will they do to King William or the Crown Prince should they ever come to London, not merely for the flogging, but for the shooting of patriotic women ?

For all these crimes and horrors, one man, Count Bismark, the most thorough incarnation of Satanic cunning, cold-bloodedness and lust of conquest since the days of Napoleon I., is responsible. It is by his Machiavellian policy and hardened, unprincipled nature, that Prussia has been led into her schemes of lawless aggrandisement. By his war on, and dismemberment of Denmark, he began, when Europe was in profound peace, the series of robberies of the smaller states around him, which excited the French Emperor to call for counterbalancing additions of territory. Bismark, from the correspondence betwixt him and the French ministers, which has come to light, had evidently been playing with the weak cupidity of Napoleon, and irritating him by such acts as that of attempting to place a Prussian prince on the throne of Spain, till he roused his indignant dupe to the temper of war : and hence all the horrors which have been exhibited before all Europe. The pretence of this man on which the war continues, that Alsace and Lorraine are necessary to the future protection of Germany, is too shallow to deceive even a child. ·The Germans have shown that any future invasion by France is absolutely ridiculous. They threw back the late attempt at invasion as a man would toss up a feather. They did not suffer the French to set a single foot on German soil ! The craving for these provinces is but a continuance of that lust of fresh territory which has been at the bottom of all the Bismarkian policy from the onset on Denmark until now.

And what a revolting spectacle is that of the old King of Prussia, a man of seventy-five years, incited by this bloodhound to a perfect mania of slaughter ! To see this old man, who fancies himself doing God service by his zeal for blood, following the army everywhere. Watching with the eagerness of novelty all the sanguinary progress of battles, and praising God for them, while he is truly realizing in himself the description of St. Paul as one of those " Whose feet are swift to shed blood. Destruction and misery are in their ways : and the way of peace have they not known. There is no fear of God before their eyes." Romans iii. 16—18. A more perfect image of Satanic infatuation cannot be conceived.

And this Frederickism in Berlin ! The very boys
inspired with it, and crowning the statue of the sangui-
nary and perfidious old Fritz with garlands, whilst the
Queen claps her hands in approbation from the balcony
of the palace ! There is a prospect for the coming
age ! Every clap of those royal hands will be felt in
the heart of fresh soldiers slaughtered ; fresh women
shot for defending their homes and loved ones ; fresh
women and children burnt alive in the blazing villages !
Well may we ask—"When is Christianity to begin ?"

*   *   *   *   *

Since I sent my MS. to England, I have seen with
the greatest pleasure in English journals, the remarks
of the great American orator and philanthropist,
Wendell Phillips, on this Franco-Prussian War. They
were so completely the counterpart of my own, that
one might be supposed to be copied from the other.
This, however, is an impossibility. Mr. Phillips can
not have seen mine, for till now they were not pub-
lished, and mine had reached England from Venice
before I happened to see his. They are, never-
theless, from the same mind, — from the universal
mind and spirit of humanity, which on both sides of
the Atlantic consigns to eternal infamy the detestable
savagery of Prussianized Germany. Sir John Lubbock
gave a lecture to the Working Men of Liverpool, during
the late Meeting of the British Association, on Savages.
He made one astonishing omission, that of the—Prus-
sians—the greatest savages that the world has ever

produced.   People have generally flattered themselves
that this war was a war of Protestantism against Catho-
licism.   An egregious mistake.   It is a war of Infidelity
against Christianity; for it is a notorious fact that
Prussia and Germany are the most infidelized and
materialized people in the world.   Their professors
teach materialism from their chairs, and more than
2,000 clergymen from their pulpits, if the disciples of
Professor Schenkell, of Heidelberg, are to be believed,
for a few years ago in Flugblätter, in my possession,
they published this statement.   " Their works do follow
them."

Wendell Phillips and Bismark.—The New York
papers contain a long letter by Mr. Wendell Phillips
on the subject of the Franco-German war, from which
we make the following extracts :—" The first step that
Prussia made from Sedan to Paris, destroyed for ever
all Bismark's claim to be thought a statesman.   Igno-
rantly or angrily, he flung away such an opportunity of
strengthening his own land in the gratitude of France
and the admiration of the world.   Instead of this, he
did all that in him lies to ensure that immortal hate
and undying purpose of revenge which will breed up
the next generation of Frenchmen for nothing else but
to put the tricolour some day over Berlin.   The next
generation of Prussia will have cause to weep that at
this hour, so great in possibilities, Prussia had no states-
man to reap the harvest which her greatest of captains
(Moltke) had got for her.   The man whom we all
thought a Sully, an Oxenstiern, turns out only to be an

adroit manager, second lieutenant to Moltke, and the willing tool of a bigot king—no breadth, no foresight, no large instinct of humanity, always the highest wisdom. Humanity itself would hardly weep if the pestilence delivered Paris, leaving neither peasant nor princeling to tell the tale at Berlin. The tears and curses of the civilized world blast the German laurels. Napoleon's fall was speedy—in less than thirty days. Prussia's is quicker still. She entered Sedan borne on the wonder, almost the loving admiration, of the world. She left it followed by the loathing and the contempt of both continents. We rejoice that Providence thus buries under its own folly this new and dreadful military power, and robs it of the means to cripple the rising democracy, as it might have done had it retained the respect of the world. Our Government should utter the verdict of civilisation and liberty on this bald barbarism. It should at least protest against this vengeance on unoffending France, this insult to the spirit of the age. The oldest republic, the master power of the next century, should speak for humanity amid this breathless and cowardly silence of kings."

For confirmation of my statements regarding the military despotism of Prussia and her aggressive spirit, with its prospects of a fatal result for Germany and Europe, let the reader see an article entitled "Bismarkism" by Frederick Harrison, in the *Fortnightly Review* for December 1st, 1870, and an article in the *Spectator*, December 31st, 1870, under the head "*Funkerism.*"

CHAPTER XI.

THE BATTLE-FIELD.

" And o'er the Earth is risen furious Hell."
Morris's Tale of Bellerophon, The Earthly Paradise.

Those whose nerves do not allow them to read what others perpetrate with indifference, not in a solitary instance, but for days, weeks, and months successively, had better pass over this chapter.

OVER the autumn fields the sun shines warmly ;

Solemn and sweet its tempered radiance lies

On the broad champaign ruddy with ripe corn.

It seems the sabbath of benignant nature,

Who has filled earth with overflowing plenty :

Working God's will for man's rich blessedness.

The peasants, men and women, are abroad,

And their glad hearts accept the dower of heaven.

And in the usual courses of the seasons

Blithely and busily the peasant people

Had garnered up the wealth which through the
  summer,
With weary frames, and tanned and reeking brow,
They had tilled and guarded,—blessing God for
  plenty.
  But now, what meaneth all this frenzied haste?
This panic mien, and terror of the reapers?
The foe is on the march! To-morrow's sun
May see him in these fields : so they rush on
To save their harvest!—Fruitless all their labours!
  —There comes a strange wild sound. They
  stand and gaze
And see thick dust whirl up from the white roads;
And hear the crack of thongs; and through the cloud
See peasant wagons driving furiously ;
See cattle run, and hear the piteous wail
Of women and children. On and on they come,
From many quarters. Wave their hands and shout
" The foe ! the foe !" and every cheek turns pale :
And every heart beats thick ; for in the land
Has war been rumoured, though they fondly
  dreamed

8

It far away, and seeking other goal.

    Down drop their tools, and man and wife and
    child

Rush towards their homes,—the sires with ashy lips

Close pressed and livid cheeks, the wives

And children shrieking as they run.   In haste

Their horses are brought forth, their wagons set

Ready for flight : their little stock of goods

Thrown pell-mell in wild chaos on each other.

Beds, tables, clothes, provisions snatched in haste.

And backward still they glance—The foe ! the foe !

They see the distant line of black invasion,

And onward rush with bleeding hearts, and eyes

That turn and mark what they would fondly save.

And cast a last wild look on all they love,

And ne'er will see again.   That dear old home !

Those barns and stalls, and fruit-bent orchard trees ;

The very house-cat mewing grievously ; the doves

Wheeling in dread around : all, all so dear

From childhood, to their fathers all so dear.

    But hark ! the sullen drum, the trumpets' wail,

The rush of galloping steeds ! again they fly.

Yet on the neighbouring rise, they turn and mark,
Wide as the eye can reach, a dark, dread mass,
The living sea of military death, roll on ;
A vast expanse of dense, compacted troops,
Without a visible end.   The worrying drum,
The music's clang, the banners' restless flash,
The stamp of countless hoofs, the heavier thud
And thunder-stroke of the timed tread of men—
Hundreds of thousands on their murder march !

   Faster they fly, but in a wild, mad rout
Of other jostling crowds, neighbours and friends
And strangers from far villages and farms,
Till all the roads are choked with misery :
With woe-crazed men, with bowed and sobbing
       women,
And frightened children : and the motley scene
Of household goods, cattle and trooping dogs.

   And what have all these done that they should
       fly ?
And leave their homes and fields to sudden waste ?
Nothing, but being men, they bear the curse
Of the war-madness of their maniac race.

And whither shall they fly?   For other hosts
Are meeting them, who come to mix their blood
In furious slaughter with the hosts behind.
Whither?   God only knows !   We know but this—
They speed to exile and return to ruin !

Meantime those hosts of murder-breathing men
Come marching on with music pealing wide
From all their bands ; come stepping to its notes
Gaily, as gathering to a jocund dance—
But 'tis the dance of death !   And all their banners
Devour the winds and quiver to the sun !
And fiercely neigh their chargers.   Now they halt !
The shrill-tongued trumpet speaks, and voices hoarse
Shout their commands ; and there is mustering close,
And horsemen galloping with fiery speed
Along the serried ranks—a pause—and then—
Flash forth hell's fires ; hell's thunders shake the
          earth.
From both sides bursts a din of direst shrieks
And groans and yells amid the sulphurous smoke
And flashing fires of the opposing lines
Of death's huge engines.   Men are blown to shreds,

And blood and human brains are driven far :

And mingled masses, living limbs and dead,

Are hurled in heaps, and still the fury grows !

And still for hours, ay through the terrible day,

These maniacs rush amid the infernal dark

And through the nitrous stench, with demon rage

More demon than the rancour of deep hell.

More bloodily rabid than the rabid beasts.

Incessant rains the hail from deadliest guns ;

With bayoneted ranks they madly drive

Against the living bodies of fellow men,

And ever more stupendous is the roar

Of the incessant cannon, that cut down

Whole files of life : and still the fury grows !

Here sways the reeking mass, pressed hotly back,

Then rallying, mows its gory swath anew.

And there is flight ; and there are galloping hosts

Of cavalry who dash through living heaps,

Smiting the human face divine to mud.

And through the shrieking, writhing, prostrate mass,

Come tearing the artillery's monstrous weights,

The Juggernautic cars of modern Europe—

Drawn by infuriate horses, and with crash
Of human bones and spirt of human blood,
Plough their fierce way to slaughter's carnival!
　　The man, whoever or whatever styled,
Who perpetrated but a single deed
In common life of murder such as these
Would be held infamous for evermore,
And on the gallows expiate his crime
Amid the curses of the multitude.
He who in darkling lane, or lonely wood
Should stealthily, and shuddering at his guilt,
Murder his fellow, would excite a flame
Of indignation burning through all ranks.
What then should be the infamy of him
Who for revenge, or for the lust of power,
Murders and mangles hecatombs of men,
And through whole provinces spreads death and ruin,
Were not this earth the Bedlam of the worlds?
　　At length the tempest of demoniac rage
Moves onwards, and the sun reveals its work.
Horrible! monstrous! indescribable!
No human tongue or pen can tell the tale

Of what this human madness perpetrates.

For miles on miles the battered earth is heaped

With men alive and dead; the living oft

Smothering in gore, and crushed beneath the dead.

Horror in all its forms is there : a thousand limbs

Torn from their trunks, and scattered in red heaps,

And severed heads, and faces shot away.

And noble horses, by the will of man

Brought to this hell of horrors, with wild shrieks

Make still more dread the shrieks and groans of men.

    The ground is gore : the trees are splashed with
        gore :

The streams and furrows run with blackening gore.

The horror of the scene has never had.

Its likeness in the realms of wrath below.

Men, horses, arms, whelmed in promiscuous heaps,

The gaunt machines of ruin crushed themselves

Lie splinter'd fragments in the general wreck.

    The homes and barns of the fled peasant bands

Have vanished in the flames of bursting shells.

Their sites are smouldering heaps of smoky stones.

But where are the destroyers ?   They have not

Mounted into the air ; have not gone out
Like a tornado, or a thunder-crash.
They still march onward, bearing to fresh scenes
Their labours of destruction.   In their hands
And in their hearts the curse of desolation.
Behind them stalk the spectres of despair.

    But through this deadly track the ambulance
And litter are busily moving, and sad hands
Sort out the sparks of life in the vast death.

    Oh ! men who glean thus wofully the fields
Of fierce destruction's harvest, ye have need
Of nerves of steel, and hearts in which the pulse
Of love beats strongly 'mid the strength of heaven ;
For to your eyes and ears come sights and sounds
So full of agony, so charged with griefs,
Come such accumulations of despairs,
That madness must assault you in your rounds
If ye are not unsouled automata
Or knights invincible of holy duty.

    What torturing pangs, what patience must be yours
To hear the incessant cries of " Water ! water !
For God's sake water ! for I burn ! I die !"

To see the bleeding arm stretched out for aid ;

To meet the pleading and pathetic eye

Of him who cannot speak ; to lift and save

Yet leave ten thousand others to their fate.

To hear the piteous cries—" Oh leave me not !

By all that's holy save my sinking life !"

And yet to know that, spite of every succour,

Of every strained and resolute exertion

Of hastening bands of helpers, there shall lie

Thousands at night on that accurséd field,

Who never shall see morning.   Their swift blood

Shall carry forth their souls.   That through the dark

Hundreds in burning agonies shall roll

And through the tardy-creeping hours shall think

Of all they love in homes far, far away,

And know that they shall never see them more !

Ay, that on such grim fields, or in lone woods,

Not for a day or night, but days on days

And nights on nights; shall wasting wretches lie

Praying for death, yet even Death himself

Refuse his aid to still their miseries !

Oh ! men, as ye have paused o'er some fine form

Blasted in life's exuberance ; as ye gazed
On some young face of beauty, boyish still,
Fixed in the marble of death, your thoughts
Must have flown wide, and pictured anxious hearts
Dreaming of him, and wondering of his fate—
And that was it !

            And thus do thousands lie
Whom tender love has reared from infancy ;
Whom cares and costs unstinted have built up
To vigorous manhood ; who have passed long years
In study of arts of life, or quest of science,
In acquisition of all charms that grace
Refined existence.   Who have sate and learned
In holy fanes the mysteries of God,
And of eternity and truth, and love
That bindeth man to man, and state to state ;
And dreamed in youthful dreams of high achieve-
      ments ;
Of winning grateful record from their kind,
By their beneficent, or useful deeds,—
And this the end !—a battered, bloody mass,
Amidst ten thousand such—a hasty pit—

'Mid festering carcases,—and that is all !—

Are these, ye people of these learned times !

Of these most civilized and Christian times !

Are these the works of wise and Christian men ?

Is this then all that science has achieved ;

That learning has produced in all her halls

Of proud assumption ? That the study of right

And rightful legislation : the discoveries

Of science in fire and air, in rock and water,

So boasted of, has brought ? Is it the whole

That your religion preached in all your churches,

And vaunted as the law of love and peace,

Has yielded ? Is it well that art itself,

And all the works of art and works of science,

That all the hoards of history and knowledge,

That love and brotherhood 'twixt land and land,

Should be destroyed by madness of the hells ?

Be trampled down by Satan's maniac hosts ?

Oh ! madness, hideous, inconceivable !

That falsifies all human claims to reason ;

That wraps the intellect in murderous glooms ;

That gives to demon rage the name of glory ;

That makes of man the monster of all monsters !

NOTE TO CHAPTER XI.

THE COST OF THE FIRST FIVE MONTHS OF THE FRANCO-PRUSSIAN WAR.

THE *Tagblatt* of Vienna has the following just obser-
vations : " It is five months since the war broke out
betwixt Germany and France, and three months since
the cosmopolitan city of Paris has been besieged by
the German armies. Leaving humanity at present out
of the question, let us calculate the losses in the
fallen, in the dead in hospitals, and in the mutilated, as
if they were not men, but simply machines, and we shall
see that, on the part of the Germans, the losses amount
to 200,000 men ; on that of France, to 250,000. That
is, in all, 450,000. Reckoning the least gain of these
men at 300 florins each, the two nations will have lost
by the cessation of their productive labour, and by
contingent consequences, 135 millions of florins. As-
suming that, on an average, a family of five individuals
consumes the value of 1,000 florins per annum, we shall
have 135,000 families that have lost every means of
subsistence, and consequently, the two kingdoms will
have at this moment, 675,000 persons reduced to ab-
solute beggary. But that is not all. The losses from

the cessation of the breeding of cattle, sheep, horses, etc., from the suppression of industrial and agricultural production, and from destruction and non-manufacture of utensils, etc., will be much greater than those we have indicated as occasional to men of capital, and will amount to 5,000 millions of florins ; so that the total loss occasioned by the war will exceed 6,000 millions of florins." Quoted by the Roman journal, *La Capitale*, Dec. 25.

Will mankind ever awaken to a proper estimate and punishment of these ogres of their race, sanguinary kings and ministers ? What are we to think of the King of Prussia and his Chancellor, who can persist in such a career of wholesale destruction, after having sacrificed nearly half a million of men in the two armies ? What possible advantages can they obtain from down-trodden France, even if they sack and plunder Paris, which can compensate in the very minutest degree for such a waste of human life and the material of human life ? Yet, in spite of the remonstrances, the tears and indignation of their own countrymen and women, they were, at the moment this was written, marching down another 150,000 men on France, to supply the waste of slaughter. These 150,000 men were of the Landwehr, the militia ; men, for the most part, of the middle classes, shopkeepers, manufacturers and the like, unaccustomed to the hardships of a regular campaign : married men and heads of families of from thirty-five to forty years of age, who, in what their countrymen already in the field describe as a perfectly Siberian winter, must perish wholesale by the weather if not by the arms of the enemy.

What these fresh troops may expect is only too sorrowfully indicated by telegrams like the following : " Dresden, Jan. 2, (1871). *Yesterday arrived here two convoys of Saxon soldiers who have lost their hands and feet from frost before Paris ! ! !*"

Can any emissaries from the nether regions be conceived more callous to human misery than the King and minister who witness such horrible sufferings of their own people, and persist in still inflicting them, to say nothing in general of their destruction of human life, wealth, happiness, and civilization ?   Were not this world insane beyond imagination, men with so hideous a development of the organ of murder would be at once seized and shut up for ever.   Whoever does not denounce such men, participates in their crimes and reponsibilities both to this and all future generations.

A German paper early in January (1871) gave these statistics.   In Hanover there are declared, on competent authority, to be 28,000 widows, and 52,000 orphans made by the war ; in Westphalia, 13,140 widows, and 29,428 orphans ; in the Hanseatic towns, 8,312 widows, and 14,715 orphans.   Total 49,452 widows, and 96,143 orphans.   These figures, which include only three provinces, are not complete even in them, as they represent only such families as have demanded succour from the government and the communes.

CHAPTER XII.

THE WORKERS IN THE RUINS.

GLORY and praise immortal unto them
The better, saner, more compassionate bands,
Who in the track of murder promptly spring,
To soothe and bind and heal, if but in part ;
And oh ! how small a part is left to them !
 Ye kindly souls, ye dear and merciful !
Ye save us from the clutch of deadliest doubt ;
Ye pluck the faith-destroyer from our hearts ;
Ye show us that our holy faith is fact.
In you the truth of Christ stands manifest,
In its celestial love and martyr zeal.
The mark which Christ has set upon his own—
By this shall all men know ye "my disciples
That ye love one another :" that is yours !

Ye gather in all lands the needful means ;

Ye flock in fearless faith, into the haunts

Of battle, 'mid the groans of shattered men.

Ye carry there your therapeutic skill;

Ye feel no fear of the contagious breath

Of pestilence ; of sights to wring the soul

And shock the delicate senses.   The soft hands

Of pitying women soothe the fevered head,

The burning wound, the torture of the mind

That sees its future life a living death ;

Its hopes destroyed, its usefulness struck down ;

Its fate to steal through life a crippled shade.

Glory and praise immortal unto you !

    And yet—dear friends, amid your noble toils,

Does it not steal upon your musing minds

That though ye have done well, there yet remains

Behind far better ?   That though bravely done

To heal and mend the ravages of war,

'TWERE BETTER, OH ! FAR BETTER TO PREVENT

    THEM !

    Ah ! when your best is done, how infinite

Is the dread sum of what ye cannot do !

Ye cannot wake the dead whom war has slain,

Cutting them down in all the glow of life.

Ye cannot heal the broken bleeding hearts

That in ten thousand bosoms weep their loss.

Ye cannot call those sons and brothers back,

Nor sires of countless orphans, who must wrestle

With the wild blasts of time without their shield.

Ye cannot build again the vanished homes ;

Nor till the stripped and desolated fields ;

Nor bid their orchards bloom and bear anew ;

Ye cannot, by the magic of good-will,

Erect once more the war-bombarded cities :

Build up their towers and spires and ruined houses :

Give to their streets and shrines the proud memorials

At once, of ancient art and famous men.

Ye cannot fill the shelves of libraries

With all the mental wealth of learnéd ages ;

With all the records of their thoughts and acts,

Which vandals have destroyed.   Much less can ye

Call back the armies of departed souls,

Sent by their rulers in the storm of hate,

In the malignant flame of baleful passions,

Drenched with the sacred blood of brother men,
To the mysterious spheres of the eternal.

These things ye cannot do, but ye can do
Far greater—ye can stanch the world's huge wound.
With all your love's devotion, ye have still
To scale a nobler height.   Ye are not yet
High on the Jacob's ladder of God's truth,
The foot of which is in the woes of earth,
But its bright summit in the halls of heaven ;
Upon whose top stands pitying God himself,
And on whose radiant steps the angels pass
Upward and downward for the love of men.
Ye cannot change the past, ye can the future.

Ye can cry " Halt !" to wars incarnadine
And wasteful waves—" Hitherto and no further !"
Ye can pronounce the thunder-burst, whose shock
No power of demon, kaiser, king or priest,
No combination of perverted counsels
Can hear, resist, and live.   That mighty word
Which intuition of all times has named
Voice of the People ! voice divine of God !

Ye statesmen, pastors, learned and unlearned ;

Ye tradesmen, husbandmen and mechanists ;
Ye lawyers, doctors, orators and writers ;
Ye thinkers in your closets, and ye workers
In mines and populous factories and shops ;
Ye who, all swart and broiling, urge the fires
Of blinding furnaces ; who midst the din
Of wheels and ponderous hammers, and fierce steam
Labour ; or guide the rushing train ; or pile
Aloft great buildings ; or do ably steer
Ships through all oceans, or on mountains tend
Your solitary herds ; or till our plains
With ever-during and prolific patience—
Men in whatever mystery, or art,
Or under whatsoever guise, or name,
Ye live and speak—the manhood of the nations—
And ye, our sisters in all lands and ranks,
Princess or peasant ; heirs of wealth and beauty,
Or ye who toil with sad, submissive souls
Beneath the withering sun or freezing sky,
Or in great cities' multitudinous dens.
Ye who are called to clothe the mind with know-
    ledge

Or to ameliorate woes; ye happy mothers,
Sisters and loving friends, to whom is given
To mould and fashion childhood's plastic soul—
Ye, one and all, in the collective strength
And sovereignty of man—'tis yours to speak
The high command that—WAR SHALL BE NO MORE!
  God has now shown in bloodiest spectacle
The madness of the nations.   He has let
The prince of evil breathe the venom of hate
Through mighty peoples, till they have rushed forth
To mutual butchery, rioting in death,
And hewing down a total generation
Of youth and vigorous manhood;
Strewing whole regions with their mangled limbs;
Destroying all the wealth and works of peace;
Giving the lie to all our lofty claims
Of civilization and of Christian love.
Mad must he be who would not stem this madness!
Who will not lend a hand to chain the brute
Which has within us raged so long, and let
The godlike in us rise and be enthroned.
  The savage only reasons with his fists,

The wise man reasons only with his reason.

And we have been mere savages too long.

Our interests, our welfare, all our hopes

Call us to listen to the Man Divine.

And found his reign on earth—One Brotherhood.

There is no plea of wrong, however monstrous,

That e'er can justify resort to arms ;

For there can be no wrong so gross and terrible

As war's collective curse of every crime,

Of every violence, offence and death.

Hail to you then, ye men of the great mass,

Ye workers and producers, who now stretch

Your friendly hands across contending nations

Towards each other in a league of peace ! *

And abjure war for ever.   Hail to you !

Ye who through weary ages were the dupes

And hopeless victims of dynastic power ;

Ye whose forefathers have made fat the earth

With their red blood, shed for the whims of kings ;

* See the circular of the Working Men's International
Associations of France, Germany, and England, in the news-
papers of September, 1870.

Ye who shall soon ascend the heights of strength
With minds enlightened, and with well trained wills,
And in your turn shall dictate to the world.

Hail to you, infinite Concourse !   By your vow
Ye wrest the weapons from the regal hands,
And break the sword, and turn the stuff of war
Into the aliment of popular weal.

And hail to you, Freemasons of the land
Of noblest liberty, fair Switzerland !
For ye too have abjured this curse of men,
And for yourselves renounced it and its sin. *

Hail watchers of the prophet, who now cry
"What of the night ?"   And the loud answer comes
In popular acclaim —" The Morning dawns !"

So, this is the beginning prayed for long,—
The dawn of common sense, the end of kings,
If kings cannot be sworn to keep the peace.

Stand forth then, all ye men of state and name !
Stand forth, and bow your necks unto the truth.

* See the Manifesto of the United Freemasons of Switzer-
land, published in the "Neue Züricher Zeitung," September
17th, 1870.

Ye statesmen, learn to bind and not to sever;

In unity seek glory; and let your minds

Bend all their faculties to cherish peace

As much as ye have strained them after war.

Ye legislators, leave your mountain pile

Of little laws, and pass one glorious act

Stamping all war as infamous for ever:

That whatsoever monarch shall seek war;

Hint but its very wish, shall stand deposed.

The act itself shall be his fixed dethronement.

Ye ministers, so named of Christ the Blest,

The Prince of Peace, the Lord of perfect Love,

No longer preach His word with hollow faith,

But in its grand concreteness speak it out:

And tell your flocks that war and strife are cursed.

There is no strife, there can be none in Christ!

There is but love, and His are known by love;

And to destroy and ravage are not love.

Oh! had ye stood, ye heralds of the Lord,

Planted in every parish, every church,

And meeting-house throughout the so-called lands

Of Christendom, and spoken out the word

Of Christ's own truth as He has left it you,
Wars had ceased utterly this thousand years.

But ye have been made blind by earthly creeds,
And by school logic warped and stupefied ;
And have paid far more homage unto these—
To canons, rituals and gross ceremonies,
Than to the central and foundation truth
Of perfect peace, and perfect love of neighbour,
And perfect union of all mankind,
Ordained by word and ratified by deed
Of your eternal King and lawgiver ;
Or worse, ye have stooped low your well-fed backs
Like Issachar betwixt the puzzling burdens
Of this world and the other, and become
Servants to tribute, traitors to your Lord.

And so this dreadful plague has raged through
time,
And the world now demandeth at your hands
Your brothers' blood through all these generations.
Rouse ye then, stand to the eternal truth
As the first Christians stood, and shout aloud
" They who shall fight and slay are none of Christ's."

And haste ye, for by multitudes already

The truth ye should have welded on the world

Is being uttered, nay, the stones themselves

Of the great highways will cry out ere long

And shame you, if ye further hold your peace.*

And, finally, ye tender-hearted women,

Whose tears have rained so on the wrecks of war :

Who have so striven to mend and piece the limbs

That barbarous war has shattered. Who have seen

That even to the few in part restored,

Ye could not give the severed hand, or foot,

The radiant eye, the once so buoyant heart,

The freely breathing chest, and the light frame

Exulting lately in its manly power.

If ye will save the coming time from grief,

From dreadful desolation, wounds and deaths,

From international hates and crimes like these,

Ye must resolve that WAR SHALL BE NO MORE !

No more must wake the demon of destruction

By gift of drum or trumpet to your child :

Must never more embroider gaudy banners

* See p. 139.

To lead the hosts of death unto their prey.
Never by hero-praise, or songs of war
Prepare the blood-bath of the coming age.

Swear never to unite your fates with men
Whose trade is blood.   Never more let your hearts
Dance at the sound of music which means death.
Never more enter churches where Te Deum
Is chanted to the God of all mankind,
To the good Father for his children slain !

Remember, it is your especial grace,—
That ye are for this special work created,
To be the springs of love, and heirs of love—
And woe to you if you betray your trust,
And yield your holy charge to the Destroyer !
Shout, therefore, in the universal shout
Of suffering nations—" WAR SHALL BE NO MORE !"

NOTE TO CHAPTER XII.

WORKERS AMONGST THE RUINS.

Note, page 137, line 5—

And shame you, if ye further hold your peace.

I need scarcely say that in this strong condemnation of the ministers of the so-called Christian church, I condemn no one for not acting beyond his lights ; but sincerely respect and sympathize with all conscientious souls who have acted up to them. It is obvious, however, that the Christian church, so-called, has never yet fully and fairly accepted and practically preached and acted out the plain truths of Christ's gospel. This we owe to the spirit of priestcraft early introduced into the churches from Pagan and Jewish sources. Its fruits are before the world in nearly two thousand years of the reign, not of Christ, but of Moloch. It is a most extraordinary fact, that with the most luminous and unmistakable words and acts of Christ before them, the churches, both priests and laity, have gone on professing full faith in Christ, yet treating him practically, either as an impracticable dreamer, or as a Father of Lies. For whilst he has imperatively forbidden his

followers to return evil for evil, but to love even their
enemies, and do good to those that hate them, he has
also said in terms as plain—" Those who believe in me
shall never be forsaken."

Nothing but the Satanic power of the most extra-
ordinary madness involved in the fall of man, can
account for a conduct in the churches so directly op-
posed to the divine commands read in them every
week : and that, with the exception of Fox, Penn,
and the Friends as a body, no church has yet dared to
put practical faith in these commands and assurances.

I cannot refrain from here drawing attention to an
admirable letter signed by " A Member of the Society
of Friends," which appeared in the *Times*, December
8th, in which the writer replies to " sharp and un-
merited charges brought against the Quakers in an
Article entitled ' England Shutting-up,' in *Blackwood's
Magazine* for December, 1870." He considers that the
report in that day's *Times* of a meeting convened at
the Mansion House by the Society of Friends in aid
of the war victims, was in itself refutation sufficient of
the charges brought against the Quakers that " the
lazy Quaker shirks military service and public duty,
and tries to escape public burdens, that he may give
himself up to ease and the accumulation of wealth ;
that he throws on other men all the hard and danger-
ous work of the world, and thrives at their expense,

isolating himself from their interests, passions, and fortunes, and lives only to his own sect." The writer observes that "a more inaccurate paragraph than the above it would be difficult to pen," and then runs over the names and labours of the Frys, the Sturges, the Fosters, the Lancasters, the Hodgkins, and the Fowlers, whose philanthropic works within the last half-century have in no inconsiderable degree helped on the progress of European civilization; draws attention to the aid, both personal and pecuniary, rendered by the Society of Friends during the Irish Famine and Lancashire distress, and to "the scores of thousands of pounds contributed by them for the starving freedmen of America, as well as for the war victims in Finland, previously on a smaller scale." Then with regard to the present crisis, he gives the interesting information obtained by calling at the central office of the Friends' War Victims' Committee, 84, Hounsditch; that up to the date of his letter, the sum of £16,827 (the Society of Friends consisting of about 15,000 members) had been received at that office for the war victims, in addition to very large contributions in the form of clothes, blankets, &c., irrespective of considerable sums known to be otherwise contributed; and that the great bulk of this sum had been subscribed by the Quakers themselves. Upon which he observes that "had all other denominations in the land raised a proportionate sum (more than £1 per head) the total would have been some thirty millions." Nor was the aid afforded by the Friends alone the gift of money,

but he found that they "had formed in most towns in
the kingdom, committees for making clothes for the
victims, whilst eleven gentlemen and four ladies had
proceeded to the seat of war, personally to superintend
the distribution of these contributions, these gentle-
men and ladies giving their services gratuitously, even
their travelling expenses being paid for by themselves
or friends, and not out of the funds collected for
the victims. And one of these gentlemen he heard
had been prostrated by small-pox in the midst of his
arduous labours." The writer concludes his letter by
saying—" It is because the sufferings of war are so
extreme and as they (the Friends) consider so need-
less, that they unceasingly seek to prevent all wars:
and while they admit the sincerity and heroism of
many who are willing to take up arms in what is
deemed a righteous cause, the Friends hold *that it may
be a yet higher heroism to obey, at the risk of any
sacrifice, even of life itself (and perhaps under circum-
stances destitute of the sustaining excitement and
honours of popular warfare), what they, at any rate,
imagine to be a Divine Prohibition.* But while they
shrink from the bloodshed of war, they by no means
turn away from participation in the labours of alle-
viating the sorrows, and bearing the burdens of Chris-
tian responsibility which it entails."

Again in the *Times,* January 9th, 1870, have the
Friends made a bold and noble declaration of their
peace principles.

CHAPTER XIII.

"THE HEALING OF THE NATIONS." *

IF men be true who say that wars must be,

Then Christ is false. If men be wise who say

Wars are inevitable,—Christ must be a fool.

If men are good who justify these wars,

Then Christ is evil, for his law condemns them.

But if our Lord be true, and wise and good,

Then they who war, spite of His holy word,

Are false and foolish and wicked, all in one.

And whether Christ, the Lord and Prince of Peace,

Be right, or they be, let the end proclaim

The eternal verdict : for our warring race

Raises but counter.wrath, and·counter vengeance :

Spills blood, spreads misery, desolates the earth,

And reaps but trouble and discord ; and sits down

---

* "And the leaves of the tree were for the healing of the
nations."—*Revelation*, xxii. 2.

On ashes of repentance, and on bones
Of slaughtered men ; and on a heritage
Of hates and jealousies, and future feuds.
Whilst Christ, so patient, meek, and non-resistant ;
Having borne scorn and insult as a fool,
And gone to visible death, " even as a fool"
In man's poor judgment,—rises conqueror
Of all earth's conquerors, warrior-chiefs and kings ;
And on the right hand of the Lord of Hosts
Stands the Eternal King of all true glory !

   Therefore, oh Father, fervently we pray thee,
That this great tribulation of our world,
May cease its dread dominion.   That the torrent
Of mingled blood and tears, whose turbid flow
Has run through all the ages, may be stemmed
And dried up in the beams of thy compassion.

   Oh ! rend away, great God, the fearful spell
Of madness wrought in the deep realms of hate
From our warped intellect, and let the light
Of thy own wisdom flash into our souls.
Then never more shall Satan, Father of lies,
Father of murders, witch our hearts to murder :

And turn this beauteous world into a hell
More horrible and odious than his own.

   And we forget not, Father of mankind,
That thou hast pledged thy own divinest truth,
To end this reign of earth's insanity.
Thou hast assured us that the woman's seed
Shall crush the serpent's head ; and by thy seer,
The great and eloquent Hebrew, hast declared
That the blest day shall dawn, when men relieved
From this long frenzy shall convert their swords
To ploughshares, and to reaping-hooks their spears,
And shall learn war no more.   And once again
Thy holy oracles have proclaimed, that Christ
The blest Messiah and King of Victory
Shall put down every foe beneath his feet,
And last of all, this death.   Thus do we hold
The triple seal and promise of thy grace,
The charter of our freedom from fell war.

   But when, oh Lord ! shall this be consummated ?
We know that it shall be, but years pass on,
And still we cry—How long, oh Lord, how long ?
For the great Anarch rages more and more,

10

And deadlier are his raids on human life.

Surely the cup of misery is full :

And Satan's necromancy of destruction

Has done its worst, and unto all the worlds

Shown this, the Madhouse of the Universe.

Surely thy lights of reason and of truth

No longer shall be quenched in his foul darkness :

But the clear morning of thy covenant

Shall rise and put him to eternal flight.

Surely the knowledge that now spreads amain—

The star of civilization beaming bright

Above all climes and regions of the earth,

Heralding kindlier thoughts and unities—

Shall now bring forth thy last and crowning grace,

The snapping of the spell of our long madness.

Then shall burst forth the sun of righteous heaven

With victory in his beams, and overthrow

Of every false conceit and pseudo wisdom ;

So that all earth shall stand in deepest wonder

At the dread magic of our long delusion.

The hideous dream of our wild malady

Shall vanish, and the world awake to peace.

Therefore, we cry again, Oh Lord ! how long ?
Let not our maniac planet, dropping blood,
Still roll through heaven, the scandal of the skies,
The horror of the blest. Say thou—" Enough !"
And the sick world is healed.
                      Command the day
Charged with man's sanity and health of soul,
Which thou hast named the day of a new heaven
And a new earth, wherein dwells righteousness,
At length to dawn : and it shall be a day
More glorious than the first which shone on earth.
A day of wisdom and of ten-fold strength
From bitter teaching and experience sad
Of age-long miseries. It shall be a day
Whose heroes shall not ruin and destroy ;
But shall guard life through counsel, and aspire
To win, by sacrifice of personal care
And personal safety, universal good.
The wise shall be the wholly wise, not wise
By halves, but in their perfect scope of vision
Shall comprehend the heavens as well as earth.
The scientific then shall shed the scales

Which limit their perceptions unto matter ;

And they shall penetrate the depths of life.

The affluent shall be affluent in the wealth

Of the great good which they can spread abroad

Upon their fellow-men.   The good shall be

Good in the kindliness of brotherly hearts

And not in creeds and dogmas.   Lords of land

And stately halls shall make them resonant

With happy voices and the songs of children ;

No longer cold and splendid solitudes.

    The one great thought throughout the genial globe

Of every man and woman then shall be,—

· How can I fill the minds of men with light ?

How can I swell the tide of human bliss,

And chase corroding cares from human souls ?

How soothe the pangs of sadness and privation,

In lowly hearts and life's obscurest shades ?

    Then shall the best achievements of the arts,

And of the subtlest science, and all works

Of industry combined and complicate,

Diffuse their triumphs and their noblest blessings

Not for the few, but for the myriad whole.

Then shall man's heart, no longer introverted,

Draw every benefit inward, but enlarged

And vitalized with love, shall find its joy

In brother-love, and in the joy of all.

    Speed thou this day, oh thou who lovest men,

Who art the Lord of love : and we shall sit

And gaze into earth's history in amaze,

And it shall seem the history of hell.

For never in those realms of woe and hate

Could cruellest devils deal more cruelly

With their fierce kind than men have dealt with men.

The age-long wars and savagest massacres ;

The burning sack of cities, and the screams

Of perishing wives and children ; the black deeds

Of base inquisitors,—tortures devised

With all the art and malice of the damned ;

The living holocausts of martyred saints,

And all the pressures of grim tyranny—

These shall in time be treated as gross fables,

For man's enfranchised heart shall not be able

To credit them, as deeds of men towards men.

    Oh ! then shall nature, healed and harmonized

With the harmonious spheres of higher life,
Breathe forth the richest, purest influences—
Her winds and waters utter deepest music
Without the undertone of woe and death.

Oh ! voice sublime by prophets heard of old,
"The voice of many waters." Oh ! ye streams
Leaping and surging in tumultuous life
Through iron clefts of rocks in Alpine glens,
With worlds of swelling sound amid tall cliffs,
Gladsome, sonorous music in choral power,
Thundering, or pealing anthems up to God !

Ever-exulting waters, in that day
Of man's great restitution, shall hymn forth
Diviner symphonies to human ears.
And the free winds shall mingle their accord
In the sublime hosannas of the earth.
For Christ the Healer shall have purged the curse
From men and nature, and the ancient times
Shall be again. And God shall walk once more
Not visible, but felt through all his works.

And ever in his path shall blessings spring—
Beauty, abundance and divinest grace.

The husbandman shall sow and reap his harvests,

And fear no maniac host of soldiery

Led by some bloody king in name of God,

To lay his plenty waste.   And wonder great

Shall fill the souls of all the toiling tribes

Of agricultural life, at the vast yields

And richest quality of fruit and corn.

    The herdsmen, and the shepherds on broad plains,

Or in the airy fields 'mid Alpine clouds,

Shall catch once more entrancing cadences

Of unimagined songs ; and heavenly shapes

Glimpsing from woods ; or in the clear night air

As in the days of the primeval world.

    And everywhere in field and pathway side

Familiar, the glad eye shall pause on tints

Of wondrous beauty in the homeliest flowers,

And wonder at the magic which each leaf

Puts on, as from volition of its own :

And at the odorous life that, morn and eve,

Steals like a spirit on the twilight air.

    The atmosphere shall wear a richer blue,

And stars burn kinglier, and the very clouds

Take shapes and hues of heaven's most mystic
glories.
Far on the measureless, waste and weltering seas
A presence divine shall meet the lonely ships,
The pilgrims of the ocean, journeying sedate,
From day to day, cut off from sight of man,
And yet for men with precious freights in charge.
And there shall breathe a blessing in the winds,
And every heart shall praise the passing God.

And in all cities, ever-springing arts,
Shall as by miracle evolve, with means
Of marvellous transit, and exchange of mind ;
And happier modes and ornaments of life
Shall, in inventive, vivid intellects,
Burgeon and blossom to exuberant wealth.
Genius shall march with a sublimer step,
And strike its fires of coruscating life
Into new models of supremest beauty,
Fresh as young planets from the vast unknown.

Nor shall the human heart lag on its course
Behind the vigorous spirit.   It shall beat
With more magnanimous and generous pulse ;

And every thought shall be a glad embrace

For brother men.   Its tendencies shall be

As broad and cordial as they once were mean

And base and selfish.   It shall be baptised

With dews of heaven, and heaven itself shall draw

Nearer and clearer to its consciousness.

So that the world of spirit and of sense

Shall mingle, and the two shall be as one,

But for the veil of matter, which itself,

As the interior being grows more pure,

Shall melt, and show diaphanous, and scarce

Shut out the view of God's more wondrous realms.

Thus harmonized, thus glorified shall earth

No longer use the phrase of "here below,"

But find itself aloft in central space

With heavens above, heavens sidewards and beneath,

And having kindred claims and hopes with all.

And thus with God's and Christ's united tides

Of life and love immortal streaming down

Through unobstructed heavens, our blessed race

Shall chew no more the bitter herbs of creeds ;

Shall need no separate fane in which to worship,

But every house and every hour of time,
Each workshop and each field and lonely mountain,
Shall be the holy of holies unto God :
And from them gushing prayers and songs of praise
Shall rise a living, ever-fragrant incense,
And men shall need no teaching, all shall know
Their common Lord and Father, even the least.

And thus this once dark planet shall roll on,
Through the glad skies a ransomed paradise,
And from all lands and families and tribes
Shall rise one glorious anthem—" Praise the Lord !"

This is thy promise, God of surest truth,
We look on it, and then on what we are.
We see earth's madness and its murder-hosts ;
And boundless wretchedness, and soul-blind men,
And kneel and pray with sorrow-blended faith—
Remember, gracious Lord, thy holy word,
And haste, and let thy great salvation come !

MINOR POEMS.

THE HYMN OF NICHOLAS OF THE ROCK.

Nicholas von der Flüe, or Nicholas of the Rock, is the most celebrated Hermit of Switzerland; he died in 1487, near Sachseln, in Underwalden, not far from Stans. His contemporaries blamed him for retiring from his family into solitude; but from his cell at Ranft he dispensed the wisest counsels, and the greatest benefits to his countrymen. His noblest action was that of reconciling the contending heads of the Swiss confederation, who having triumphed over all their enemies, Burgundy, France, and Austria, were about to turn their fratricidal swords against each other. For this patriotic deed his country has enshrined his memory in its inmost heart, and placed his name on one of the proudest pages of its annals. The fame of Nicholas spread over all Europe. Popes, kings, and bishops honoured him; sent greetings to him, amongst whom was the celebrated Cardinal Charles Borromeo, who, as well as others of them, visited him. But the pen which has recorded his beneficent deeds has omitted to reveal the thoughts which were their source. May we not, however, divine them?

I DWELL alone, yet not alone.

The deep wood has a living tone.

Like thought enmassed through vastest years
The still, gray rock its front uprears.
All livid, gashed and scarred with time
It seems to stand in trance sublime.
Impassive, yet all ear and eye
It speaks to me in passing by.
The breeze that through the forest flits
Some half-caught, whispered word emits.
The earth beneath me is not dead :
It thrills and answers to my tread.

   Is this then, Nature ! thy repose ?
Ah ! every tree its functions knows.
How deeply slumberous look these hills !
What peace profound the woodland fills !
Yet nature's grass-enwoven vest ;
These foliaged glades that seem all rest ;
And all the flowers of heath and hill,
Are working, working, working still !

   'Tis all one scene of quivering life !
'Tis all with busiest action rife !
Throughout the host of giant boles
The fire of life for ever rolls.

The myriad, myriad grassy blades
A soul of subtlest art pervades :
And frames, creates in potence mute
The miracles of flower and fruit.

These waters have a voice and sight ;
They laugh and leap into the light.
These little waves, transfused with sun,
That to the strand so gaily run,
They live ! and in the tempest's hour
Will rise and thunder in their power.

Oh sky ! that seem'st a shining face,
Yet art the spirit of all space ;
Oh ! mountains old which stand and seem
To dream one deep eternal dream,—
Yet call your lightnings forth and flame
Athwart the gulfs that rend your frame,
And launch the thunder, bellowing dread,
Through night's pavilions overhead.
Oh ! all ye living things that tell
Nothing of that in which ye dwell,
Or dwells in you : that ne'er reveal
A trace of what ye know and feel ;

Ye countless creatures of each zone

That live with man, yet live alone.

That suffer, groan, and bear from him

Gigantic wrongs in patience dim.

That claim a life of head and heart

Yet keep your thoughts from men apart.

   Oh ! all thou mighty breathing sphere

Which art so far and yet so near :

Ye moon and stars and light of day—

What is it that ye strive to say ?

What is this vast and varied show

That man still sees yet cannot know ?

This congregation of all forms—

Ye winds, and floods, and frosts and storms—

Ye atom shapes, ye creeping things,

And all the family of wings :

The spring that comes with tears and sighs,

And seems to woo us, yet denies ;

What is this mystery dark and old,

That all would tell, yet ne'er is told ?

Ah ! shall not time, some happier year

Unloose this burden and make clear ?

Hark ! a soft voice suspends my will—
I sit, and wonder, and am still.
And hear a speech so low yet strong,
Say " Man finds not who seeketh wrong."

Ah ! now my scales of darkness fall !
'Tis GOD who lives and moves in all !
That life which streams from stars and suns ;
That life which through all nature runs ;
Which climbs where man has never trod,
Is God, the all-pervading God !

'Tis God whose potence underlies
This scheme of wondrous mysteries :
Through central depths, in seas and hills
With pulse eternal beats and thrills.
Who wakes the winds, and rolls the spheres,
And speaks when none but Nature hears.
Who flutters in the wild bird's wings,
And is the voice of mutest things.
Who in the monad finds a place,
And fills and overflows all space,
Who through deep fire-realms holds his march,
And sits upon the rainbow's arch.

Who in the awful and the vast,
Is the dread presence of the past.

Oh ! God of holiest love and fear !
I feel thee near and ever near.
Within me, through me, round me spread,
With all thine armies of the dead :
With all thine hosts from empires far,
Who were, and are not, and yet are.

How near they flit ! how hushed they stand !
They crowd and press on every hand.
Upon my cheek I feel the breath
Of unseen conquerors of death.
The dwellers in the viewless day
Who bring us strength to keep the way
Which Christ, his saints, and martyrs trod,
To life with God—the living God ! .

Oh ! ministers of tenderest grace !
Oh ! comforters of time and space !
Ye warrior troops of God below
Who know no check and fear no foe :
.For us your watch immortal set—
With God and you we travel yet !

Then blow ye winds, ye tempests sweep,

'Tis God who guides us through the deep.

Whose banners blaze in folds sublime

O'er all the hosts of unborn time ;

Whose tides of quenchless being roll

Through every pore of Nature's soul,

And make of us a conscious part

Of his immortal, boundless heart.

Oh ! Father God, in wonders known,

I dwell with thee, and not alone !

MAN AND NATURE.

THE wrath of man, contemptible and base,
Springs from below, but Nature, thine from God !
Beauty divine is in thy violence :
Thy rage has heavenly features : for when Death
Rides on the tempest's pinions, health and good
Are in his fierce career for man at large.
Earthquakes may topple populous cities down,
And whirlwinds winnow dread destructive fires :
Or ocean storms sink fleets : but for all these
Large compensations follow to the race,
In airs salubrious that chase far away
Miasmal death ; in springs of life renewed ;
Or in most needful warnings unto vice
That life is brittle, and that God still lives.

So have we seen a nation ripe for death,

Which sate so late as queen, and proudly said

" I am, and none beside me.   I shall sit

Never as widow, or know loss of children."*

But in one moment, both of these have come !

For when God's judgment is upon a nation,

Its armies are like mist before the wind.

And when a nation sets itself to win

The curse of God, by swiftness to shed blood,

Its armies too, are fires of self-destruction,

Which one day shall consume its strength to ashes,

And desolation shall appoint her hour

In God's own time—the scourger of .the scourge.

* Isaiah, xlvii.

Perhaps the fate of no nation was ever so completely fore-told as that of France, by the prophet Isaiah in the whole of the xlviith chapter.   Besides the coincidences mentioned in the text of these verses, her destruction was to come in her per-fection.   She trusted in wickedness : desolation was to come suddenly ; she could not tell whence, and she certainly did not expect it from Germany.   She was to be wearied " in the multitude of her counsels," and surely, never were there such divisions of parties, and opinions.   Her counsellors were to be as stubble, set on fire : no one could deliver her ; and the merchants, England and other countries, with whom she had laboured, it is said, "shall wander, every one to his own quarter ; none shall save thee." Truly, never was a nation left so utterly alone in her troubles. But what applies to one nation applies to all. France had her day of oppression of other nations : Germany has hers now : but the same seeds produce the same fruits ; the same course of action the same inevitable results.

THE HOLY SPARROW.

A JEU D'ESPRIT.

These stanzas were suggested by seeing the sparrows drink-
ing at, and washing themselves in the large brazen kettles of
consecrated water suspended in the cemetery at Lucerne—
vessels so familiar to travellers in Catholic countries.

A SPARROW lived in a cemetery,
    And a knowing bird was he ;
He was jolly, and he was wary,
Sober in garb, but brisk as a fairy,
    He lived with his family.

Daily a feast of crumbs he found
    Dropped by infant son and daughter,
Whom nurses brought in their daily round ;
And he ate, and he frisked with many a bound,
    And he drank of the holy water.

He drank, and he bathed in the holy pan
    That hung by the convent wall;
And through him the oddest sensations ran :
He imagined himself a holy man
    Aye, the saintliest of them all.

So into the Capuchin's hoary fane
    When mass was loudly chanted,
He flew, by chance of a vacant pane,
And gazed on the brown-robed brethren, and fain
    Would have told them what he wanted.

Which was to become a holy brother
    And confess the sinful people ;
But they kept up such a canticle-pother,
That out he flew—for he saw no other
    Way—and he sate on the steeple.

He sate, and thought, and it grew quite clear
    That he was a monk already.
'Tis the Capuchiner frock that I wear,
The colour's the same, and I've just the air
    Of a brother so plump and steady.

My holy waters in pans abound ;
  With tail and fluttering wings
I can sprinkle the water all around,
And bless the people, and bless the ground,
  And absolve all living things.

So this holy sparrow did duly go
  To the Capuchiner Convent ;
And when the choir was in full flow,
He sung above, as they sung below,
  And was part of whatever on went.

And a wondrous fame of him was spread,
  Wherever a chirp was heard ;
And his sanctity grew, and the sparrows said
The holiest sparrow that ever was bred
  Was this very Capuchin bird.

And when the sparrows homeward came
  From the farmers' corn-fields flying,
With crops distended they felt no shame,
For this sparrow-priest did straight proclaim
  They need have no fear of dying.

For he gave perfect absolution
　From every sin of thieving ;
And they found it an excellent institution ;
For every doubt a grand solution,
　Which left no conscience grieving.

And so since then the sparrow race
　Live plenteously and gaily,
No thieves are they ; know no disgrace,
For their holy fathers all sins efface,
　And make them angelic daily.

FLOW, SWEET RIVER.

FLOW, flow, sweet River,
Thou shalt find the ocean,
  Which is thy home.

Float, float, sweet Zephyr,
Through the opal air-floods :
  There is thy home.

Burn, burn, ye Starlights,
In your azure temples—
  Your home and ours.

THE TELBIN STONE.

On the highest point of the Axenstrasse, near Brunnen, on the Lake of the Four Cantons, the passing traveller sees a monumental stone by the roadside, recording the death of a young and promising English artist, the son of Mr. Telbin, the celebrated scene-painter, who fell from the lofty precipice into the lake below. The lake hereabout is said, in sounding, to have been found to be 8,000 feet deep. No bodies drowned in these depths are ever seen again, a fact common to other very deep lakes. The simple inscription on this stone is— "To the Memory of Henry Telbin, who fell from this spot whilst sketching, September 14, 1866, aged 25 years." The same inscription in German is repeated below. These verses were written as I used to take my favourite seat, morning after morning, in the pine forest just above this monumental stone, and in full view of the magnificent scenery referred to.

O ! WAN, gray stone, thus sadly set on high,
Telling thy tale to every passer-by.
Still looking down from thy stupendous cliff,
Telling thy tale to every passing skiff—

Why this appeal incessant for a woe
That came and went four fleeting years ago?
Within four years, how many myriad men
Have died ungraced by chisel or by pen !
Within four years, how many myriads tread
All unrecorded to the nameless dead !

   Sharp was the horror of the dread descent,
Wild was the parent's wail, the friend's lament,
For the young artist from my own far land
Who plunged in terror to the unknown strand.
But shall we grieve for those who in life's morn
Pass to the scenes to which mankind is born ?

   Life here at best is but the anchored stay
Of some strange bark which comes, and sails away.
But who, like this young Telbin, lies in state
Which kings might envy, conquerors emulate ?
No tomb like this did ever genius plan,
Or nations raise to some immortal man.

   A thousand fathoms deep his bones repose
In Mystery's Fane, which no intrusion knows.
No mortal glance shall there for ever fall ;
No mortal hand shall lift the sleeper's pall.

For ever and for ever—or while Time

Holds his for ever—Nature's chant sublime

Shall peal above him ; winds and waves intone ;

The rushing avalanche fall with shuddering moan,

And thunders answer from their summits lone.

Still the tall pines their murmured requiems sing

And odours breathe from all the flowers of spring.

And summer still the awful cliffs shall gem

With the red radiance of the lily's stem.*

    Vast are the crystal chambers of his shrine

And roofed above with purest hyaline.

And the huge mountains, in their mantles hoar,

Keep deepest, wordless watch for evermore.

    The dead ? who calls him dead who never died ?

Who only passed unto the other side.

Life has no pause, the soul no rifted chain,—

So ancient seers and modern truths maintain.

To other lands the artist's gifts belong ;

In other lands the poet hymns his song;

---

* The inaccessible parts of these cliffs are richly blossomed over in June with the orange lily of our gardens.

And on far loftier themes, with nobler fire

Than Raphael knew, or Milton did inspire.

To the dead leave the dead—'tis ours to climb

Through heights of life, to life yet more sublime.

The sons of God no chance or change surprise.

Onward they march through kingdoms of the skies.

Great pilgrims of the ages—radiant bands

Before whose feet the eternal still expands !

For ever and for ever !—Hark ! they call—

On to life's source—where Love is All in All !

THE GREAT, DISHONOURED NAME.

Oh ! holy, holy, holiest name !

Thou mark of glory and of shame !

Name which in heaven's supremest sphere

The hosts of God in transport hear ;

At whose remotest whisper dim

Bow low the glorious seraphim :

Bow all the potentates and thrones,

Through all the vast, eternal zones ;

The countless armies of God's might ;

The hierarchies of dazzling light :

Archangels strong and crownéd peers,

Kings of the far immortal years,

Spirits of wisdom whose high reach

Of knowledge mocks all force of speech ; ·

Most glorious souls, most spiritual flames,

Whose thoughts are lightnings, and whose names

Pealed round the invisible throne are heard

As thunders of the incarnate Word—

Name which art law, and life, and love,

Felt, honoured, blest, obeyed above,

With ardent soul, with prompt accord,

Through all the kingdoms of the Lord.

    Name which on this base earth art found

Still but a mockery and a sound.

Which all pretend of right to claim—

Their chartered and illustrious name,

Monarch and noble, sage and saint

With banners broad and scutcheons quaint,

Vaunting this glory as their own

But slaves to their proud wills alone;

With not one tinge from Christ's dear side ;

By not one law to Him allied ;

By not one single virtue known

As those whom he will hail his own !

    Oh ! soul-eyed, mighty seers of old

Through whom our Lord his story told ;

12

Who by the Godhead's hand divine
Limned every feature's sorrowing line,
Traced with the Spirit's fiery pen
His love, and all the wrongs of men.—
How perfect in its sombre glow
Still stands that chronicle of woe !

By men rejected, mocked, forlorn,
On Him was heaped all mortal scorn ;
Who bore our sorrows, sins, and shame,
Wronged in his spirit and his name.
Whatever human pride could dare,
Or bigot hands in hate prepare—
Whatever malice could conceive,
Or priestly cunning darkly weave,
Or treason act, or falsehood plan
Fell on the sorrow-freighted man ;
Closed round him in demoniac strife,
And slew him, though the Lord of Life.

And still through all the ages down
He wears the thorn-encrimsoned crown.
Still those who fawn and bend the knee
Heap on his head their infamy.

They kill and steal, they reek with gore
More rankly than the kings of yore ;
More pagan than rude hordes who saw
Vengeance but as dark nature's law,
And the proud hierarchs of their creed
Give Gospel sanction for the deed.
And charge their violence on Him
Who sits above the cherubim ;
And weeps the woe, and feels the shame
Cast by these traitors on his name.

    For still they kneel before his seat
And still his hallowed words repeat,
And boast his vassal bands to be,
And work death's work as his decree !

    Oh ! Lamb of God, how still doth shine
The lamb's meek sufferance in thine !
Meek Lamb of God ! for ever slain
From earth's foundation for our pain—
Still art thou slain from day to day
By those who stab thee as they pray.
Blest Lamb of God ! how long wilt thou
This mockery of thy name allow ?

How long shall kings and statesmen base
Tread down thy gospel in disgrace—
Boars who lay waste thy vineyard blest,*
Wolves in thy flock's own fleeces dressed ?
How long shall pride with withering eye
Scowl on thy meek ones passing by ?
And lust, and avarice and power
Before thy shrines obsequious cower,
And thy blest cross aloft display
Whilst marching their own headstrong way ?
And the smooth hypocrite pretend
To be thy special child and friend ?
Ah ! hence thy faith is drooping low !
This is thine altar's overthrow !
Through this thy temples, laws and lore
Are scorned and doubted more and more.
And the world's wise ones to the crowd
Proclaim their creed of death aloud :
And boast ere long thy name to cast
To the pale fictions of the past.
Lord ! shall this stand till men complain
That thou hast lived and died in vain ?

* Psalm lxxx. 13.

No, not in vain ! for thou art known
Where'er man's hopes are overthrown.
Where'er the human heart is low ;
Wherever breathes a child of woe ;
Where none besides thee aid extend—
There art thou Saviour, guide, and friend.

In many a fane that pride has built,
There prostrate falls repentant guilt.
Gross superstition's gaudy shrine
Becomes through sorrow also thine.
The poor, forsaken, scorned, unknown,
Weep out their woes to thee alone ;
And hot tears wrung from sinners bowed
Dim marble floors of churches proud.

By many a wayside, lonely shrine
The care-racked bosom leans on thine.
On desolate hearths, in chambers drear,
The world-rejected feel thee near.
And sins and sorrows dark and wild
Pass—and the fallen are reconciled.

Oh ! whilst the worldly great ones claim
The glory of thy outraged name ;

And throng their gorgeous altars round
In pride of state, 'mid storms of sound,
And spread their blood-stained hands abroad
And for their rapines thank the Lord—
Thou art not there, but with the low
Whom men know not, nor care to know,
And with the splendours of thy light
Dost chase despair's fiend-haunted night.

Oh ! vain the thought that void of worth
And scant thine harvest upon earth !
For misery's children, like the sand
Of ocean, swarm on every strand—
The poor, the oppressed, the hosts who groan—
And these are thine and thine alone.
Thou draw'st them and they follow free,
For they have none who draw but thee.
And when the clouds of death divide,
And heaven's bright portals open wide,
Oh ! what a church shall stand revealed
Around thee of the crushed and healed ;
The countless, countless myriads blest ;
The heirs of heaven's eternal rest ;

Transformed, ennobled by thy grace—
The kings of light, the lords of space ;
The small of earth, the great on high,
Thy crowned ones of eternity !
  So let me, Lord, these few dark days
Steal on through life's unnoticed ways.
Far from the hostile and the proud ;
Far from the hard, unspiritual crowd :
Far from the creed-bound souls malign
Who call on thee, and are not thine.
Rather be mine the martyr's fate
To teach thy truth, and share thy fate,
Contempt and need, and death and shame,
All—save dishonour of thy name.
  Almighty Love revealed in woe,
Death's victim, lord and overthrow,
Eternal power, eternal light
Flashed through creation's farthest night ;
Earth's shame, by feet rebellious trod,
Heaven's glory, crowned and throned with God—
Dark are our days, and low the sun,
Faith droops ; her course is well-nigh run.

Peace has expired, and sanguine rage

Usurps thy promised heritage.

Oh ! send thy truth on victory's wings ;

Strike through the thrones of discord's kings—

And show,—though but for one brief hour,

Thy gospel's peace, thy gospel's power.

LONGING FOR REST.

DEAR Nature ! let me lay my cheek to thine,
And on thy mother bosom sink to rest,
For I am weary. I have travelled far,
Both through life's mazes, and through many lands,
Circling the earth, and living amongst men
Of other natures, and I fain would rest,
For I am weary. I have now grown old
Not in the nerve of spirit or of frame,
But in the freshness of the bosom, seared
Like a still verdant branch by thunder-heats.
And in life's march of death I have beheld
The comrades of my youth, the generation
With which thou didst ally me, gone before,

And round me things and thoughts which are not
  mine.

  I have fought out the fight of this hard world
Boldly and steadfastly, intent to hold
The onward, only way of truth and faith,
But waxing oft too feverish in the strife
With the perverse and loveless sons of men,
Which better had been borne in wisdom's peace.

  But now, these conflicts and these after-lights
Are all gone by, and there is twilight calm.

  And in this evening shadow I look back
And see the radiant morning in whose dawn
Thou bor'st me on thy bosom to the fields,
And spread thy glories round me like a heaven.

  Oh ! what a paradise was then thine earth !
How sweetly fell the sunlight on the hills !
How fragrant the wild rose in briery dells ;
How beautiful were all the living forms
Of tree and flower and leaf and bloomy grass :
What music rung from bird and pilgrim bee
Humming its orisons in odorous bells ;
How sweet the chant of cock and low of kine,

And song of milkmaid from the misty mead.

What a fresh spirit in the rushing wind ;

And in the circling seasons circling joy—

A world shut in by clouds of poesy ;

All other worlds unknown, nor needed there.

   The dancing blood was heaven's own streaming

      fire ;

The heart an altar-flame of buoyant life,

And the young frame elastic, spirit-winged,

Dreamed not and recked not of its mingling earth ,

Which time with strictest reckoning adds and adds

Till with its Atlas load it sinks us down.

   All round were magic lights and fairy skies,

Which nothing dimmed or marred, for change was

      bliss.

Tempests and wintry snows and iron frosts ;

The dream-like moon, the stars in stillest march,

Were but the welcome maskers in a pageant

Where all was wondrous as an angel's dream.

Death then himself was but a name to thrill

Like the feigned spectre of a Christ-night tale.

Blest time !—a memory now, and—nothing more !

But thou, dear Nature, keep'st thy ceaseless watch,
So let me rest, and thou shalt wake me soon,
With thy soft touch, and I shall see thine eyes
Beaming on mine with all their heaven of love ;
And round me my young morning risen again,
Bright as of old, and real as thyself.
And all the loved old memories shall stand there—
Parents and brothers, and the heart's first friends
Humble but precious ; and the later wealth
Of warm existence,—children, stars of joy,
Soon waning from the sight, but to the soul
For ever present ; every place and thing
That were enwoven in life's glowing web,
Restored as never vanished.

                              So no more
From out thy kingdom of the starry hills
Shall I be exiled to this orb of woe ;
This hoar Aceldama of stanchless blood ;
Made kin to Earth's fierce progeny of strife,—
Sons of the Furies, Death's assassin bands,—
Blood-hounds and tiger-packs of vampyre kings,
Howling through ages on men's track of woe !

Oh ! lead thou me far, far from their access ;
Pile up thine adamantine walls of peace,
Subtle and viewless as the crystal air,
Yet to aught base heaven-proof, impassable.
There where the weary are at length at rest ;
There where for aye the wicked cease their troubling
Broad spread the valleys of immortal life.

There is a path unknown to any fowl ;
To which no eagle's pinion ever soared :
There is a sea where never gallant ship
With wind-blown sails, and swift adventurous keel
Did ever enter.   Yet those mystic tracks
Thou know'st, dear Nature.   Thou, heaven's char-
    tered guide,
Dost lead thy charge with sure, maternal hand
To where the central city of the soul,
Planted amid the realms of starry space,
Sends forth its glory of light ineffable
Far through the kingdoms of perfected life.

City divine of Him who built all worlds !
Queen of all nations ! fortress of all strength !
Mysterious lode-star of all human hopes—

From the high watch-towers of eternity

Reaching all eyes and cheering on all hearts,

That, once enfranchised from imperious sin,

Gather, by law omnipotent of grace,

From every land and world to their one home !

There dwell thy children of the loving heart,

And Christ, the woe-crowned king, 'mid countless

hosts,

Walks with his own, insphered with truth and God.

THE END.

BILLING, PRINTER, GUILDFORD.

WORKS BY THE SAME AUTHOR.

——0——

THE RURAL LIFE OF ENGLAND.

New and Cheaper Edition, uniform with "Visits to Remarkable Places ;" with numerous Wood Engravings by BEWICK and WILLIAMS.

Square crown 8vo., price 12s. 6d.

VISITS TO REMARKABLE PLACES :

Old Halls, Battle Fields, and Scenes Illustrative of Striking Passages in English History and Poetry.

Second and Cheaper Edition ; with upwards of Eighty highly-finished Woodcuts. .

Two Volumes, square crown 8vo., price 25s.

THE HISTORY OF AUSTRALIAN AND NEW ZEALAND DISCOVERY.

The only Complete and Connected History of these Discoveries.

Two Volumes, 8vo., price 20s.

London : LONGMANS and CO., Paternoster Row.

THE NORTHERN HEIGHTS OF LONDON;

OR,

HISTORICAL ASSOCIATIONS OF

HAMPSTEAD, HIGHGATE, MUSWELL HILL, HORNSEY, AND ISLINGTON.

In One Volume, square crown 8vo., with about Forty Woodcut Illustrations, price 21s.

OPINIONS OF THE PRESS.

" Mr. Howitt's pleasant volume will be very welcome to all dwellers in the localities it describes. It so combines handbook information with literary gossip and pleasant descriptions, that it will find a favoured place upon the drawing-room table, and be a never-failing source of amusement for leisure minutes. It may be taken up and put down at any time, and will always delight with its pleasant gossip and interesting information." — *English Independent.*

" The local memories of things and persons in the outlying shores of such a vast ocean of life as London fade out of the general mind with a rapidity only equalled by that of the spread of population into the suburbs, and the consequent metamorphoses of the surface; and we thank Mr. Howitt for rescuing from oblivion, and collecting into a pleasant and readable form, many curious biographical incidents and traditionary records of the pleasant fields, heaths, and hamlets which, in place of the brick and mortar of the present, once covered the outlying districts on the northern side of London . . . . . . Mr. Howitt's volume is throughout thoroughly readable and interesting, and we can cordially recommend it as a pleasant and genial companion for the leisure hour."— *Examiner.*

"The 'Northern Heights of London' is one of the pleasantest of books. As the Author takes his reader over the ground, he acts the part of a chatty, intelligent guide, who not only tells you who lived in the old houses, and walked along the lanes and roads, but acquaints you with the history of the men and women thus mentioned, and illustrates the times in which they flourished by a rich fund of anecdote. Its discursiveness is no drawback to the interest which it awakens. There is good history, good biography, good descriptions of the country north of the metropolis—not much of any of it at one time—an attractive gossip, in fact, more pleasing than a novel. We have read the book with undiminished interest from beginning to end, and we honestly recommend it to our readers as affording the means of a few hours' mental recreation and enjoyment."—*Land and Water.*

" A book full of interest, and likely to be more appreciated even in the future than in the present. It is in substance a minute historical record of all the more important persons and events with which the northern suburbs of the metropolis have in their past history been identified. As the encroachments of brick and mortar obliterate old scenes and associations, the painstaking efforts of those who,

WORKS BY THE SAME AUTHOR.

like Mr. Howitt, have a peculiar faculty for investing them with an all but romantic charm are increasingly valuable. Hampstead, Highgate, Hornsey, and Islington, with the adjacent districts, have all been the subject of Mr. Howitt's studies and researches, and the materials thus gathered are in themselves a sufficient memorial of his earnest and enthusiastic labours. The book is not simply a record of dry facts, not a mere amplified auctioneer's catalogue, nor the rattle-paced deliverance of a showman, but a collection of biographies and narratives told in that warmhearted and genial spirit which animates all Mr. Howitt's writings. Kings and queens, chancellors and judges, clergy, puritans, commonwealth heroes and courtezans, eccentric citizens, poets and philanthropists, actors, artists, and inventors—in short, all the notables of their day and generation who dwelt in or visited the northern suburbs of London — seem to have been the object of separate and careful study. In an easy and graphic style the Author has painted the picture of each life or striking event, and photographed with it on the mind of the reader the old red-brick mansion or wayside stone, the ancient hostelry or stately avenue where they lived, met, and parted, or walked in times when individuality of character and personal distinction stood out in far bolder relief than is possible in this age of levelling up and popular enlightenment. One by one the traces of these old times are vanishing from

gaze.... The volume contains a number of woodcuts copied from old pictures of many of the most interesting places which enliven its pages. The work is both valuable as an historical record, and delightful as a well-told story."—*Morning Star*.

"No quarter of London has more interesting associations than that which Mr. William Howitt has chosen for the subject of this most happily conceived and happily written book. Scarcely any person can walk through Hampstead, Highgate, Muswell Hill, Hornsey, or Islington—the districts embraced within this work—without almost hearing the footfalls of the illustrious dead. Mr. Howitt, with vivid pen, tells you exactly where they lived, and sometimes almost recals them again to life. For ourselves, after having read and partly re-read all that Mr. Howitt has to tell us, the northern heights will possess a nearer and more human interest than they have ever possessed before.... This is the kind of talk in which Mr. Howitt indulges. He moralises also, as in this last anecdote, and the moralising, though appropriate and true, is not very pleasant, for it is not pleasant to reflect that this is a fine specimen of how nobility is acquired and rewarded in this country. But the Author also gives some pictures of the remarkable scenes, and exquisitely engraved they are. We put down this charming work, only regretting that the Author has not extended its limits."—*Nonconformist*.

London : LONGMANS and CO., Paternoster Row.

www.ingramcontent.com/pod-product-compliance
Lightning Source LLC
Chambersburg PA
CBHW020627030726
47497CB00007B/2444